A Brush with 1

A Brush with India

An artist's journey through Rajasthan, Agra and Varanasi

Linda-Marie De Vel

Dedication

To my beloved Gaston and my cherished sister Jone.
Your gift of untiring love and encouragment
allowed me to complete this book.

Acknowledgments

Thanks to my special librarian Sue Woods
and also Clem Wiggins, a doctor of words.

First published 2002
Copyright © 2002 Linda-Marie de Vel

The author asserts her moral rights in the work.

This book is copyright. Except for the purposes of fair reviewing,
no part of this publication (whether it be in any eBook, digital,
electronic or traditionally printed format or otherwise) may be reproduced
or transmitted in any form or by any means, electronic, digital or mechanical,
including CD, DVD, eBook, PDF format, photocopying, recording,
or any inforrmation storage and retrieval system, including by any means
via the internet or World Wide Web, or by any means yet undiscovered,
without permission in writing from the publisher.
Infringers of copyright render themselves liable to prosecution.

ISBN 1-877270-32-6

Hazard Press is an imprint of Hazard Publishing Limited

Published by Hazard Publishing Limited
P.O. Box 2151, Christchurch, New Zealand
email: info@hazard.co.nz
www.hazardonline.com

Printed in New Zealand

Contents

Chapter 1: New Delhi 7

Chapter 2: Shekhawati to Bikaner 22

Chapter 3: Jaisalmer 41

Chapter 4: Jodhpur 63

Chapter 5: Ajmer and Pushkar 89

Chapter 6: Jaipur and Bharatpur, Keoladeo National Park 101

Chapter 7: Fatehpur Sikri 119

Chapter 8: Agra 133

Chapter 9: Varanasi 159

Epilogue 183

Chapter 1

New Delhi

Forget the Samurai. Don't even think of King Arthur or his Knights of the Round Table. The bravest, the most noble of them all were the Rajputs of Rajasthan. Their women were exquisitely beautiful and as brave as their men. No place on earth has seen such heroism or loyalty. They were descendants of the sun, moon and the eternal flame, educated, wealthy and fiercely independent. The women of Rajasthan wear dazzling saris of ice blue, hot orange, sunrise yellow and emerald green. Camels and elephants fill the landscape. Peacocks are as plentiful as sparrows and hilltop fortresses loom out of the desert like mirages from the tales of Ali Baba.

Rajasthan was our next destination. Gaston had chosen it as the site to paint for his next exhibition. I had always wanted to see India. Neither of us thought for a moment it would change the way we thought of the world, forever.

Gaston selected Rajasthan because the area was said to be colourful and different. This is exactly what he looks for: not just lights and shadows and familiar compositions but architecture, inspiration and a sense of the exotic. Because he is an impressionist artist, his collectors always associate him with and want paintings of France. He loves to paint in France, particularly because he is passionate about the food, but an accomplished, professional artist, who has painted over 4000 canvases, wants new challenges.

Every alternate year we go on a major trip overseas and every other year Gaston has a major exhibition for which he must have about 35 new paintings. At home he works on still-life paintings. He paints flowers – sumptuous roses in summer, tulips, Iceland poppies and delicate freesias in the spring. When the flowers have finished, he may move on to depicting the many nuances of colour in a French horn or, for variety, the depths in an old Olivetti typewriter placed alongside some potted pink geraniums. He likes to paint

A Brush with India

fruit or cheeses or a string of fish, or lobsters on platters and champagne in tall glasses.

After the studio work it is time to leave our comfortable, easy lifestyle and look for new challenges. A true impressionist, an artist looking for the freshness of colour and light, always paints from life. My husband is what the French call a rescapé, someone 'rescued' from the old times. The masters who taught him at the Academie des Beaux Arts in Belgium from 1941 to 1946 were friends of Claude Monet and John Singer Sargent, Gaston is one of the few painters left who has had the opportunity, ability and courage to continue the work that is his driving force in life.

In May, he begins to prepare for the journey. Canvases are cut no bigger than the size of our suitcases so they can lie flat. Two wooden stretcher frames are made to support each canvas while he is working. Tools, staplers, a small hammer, several cardboard viewers, are collected and packed. Oil paints of the best quality are counted and collated and the tops screwed down tightly. Plane journeys, train travel, even a car can steadily work the caps loose and cause paint to leak. Mediums to quickly dry wet paint are added. Filbert brushes are checked. Plenty of boxes of tissue paper, to keep the brushes clean, fill up corners. The fold-up wooden Lefranc combined paintbox and easel is packed and its numerous screws are carefully checked. It weighs 12 kilos (27 pounds) when fully packed. Gaston has carted this box, attached by leather straps to his back, around the world several times over. Everything but turpentine is put in order and packed away. Turpentine is our first requirement in a foreign country and trying to find it in the highlands of an Ecuadorian volcano, or in the sizzling hot bazaars of Bali, has been a hilarious and sometimes frustrating test of language and endurance.

Gaston never worries about the possibility of getting sick. Nor does he care about accommodation or require it to be pre-booked. We book only our flights in advance. We know we have to keep our expenses reasonable because we are sometimes away for five months and money disappears quickly. We stay in small hotels, usually those patronised by the locals. The only thing that does worry my Belgian husband is the quality of the food.

New Delhi

After 12 hours flying from Auckland, New Zealand, we reached Singapore, the threshold of our journey to India and our last connection to New Delhi. Sitting next to me in the airport lounge and also waiting to board the plane, was a petite Indian woman. She wore a beautiful iridescent pink silk sari, its hem heavy with gold embroidery. At her throat were several layers of gold necklaces. Bracelets on her arms made small tinkling noises when she moved. She wore delicate, pink high heels with little straps. Her hair was black and long, her eyes very dark with long lashes. I, on the other hand, looked like a pregnant duck in my long navy blue skirt, my oversized white shirt (hiding my money belt) and flat brown sandals.

I don't know what I expected from Air India. Perhaps some incense burning when we got on the plane or an alcove with the roly-poly figure of the elephant-headed god, Ganesha? It would have been appropriate, as he is the one to ask for success in life's ventures. Aside from rogan Josh, that wonderfully flavoured lamb dish, it was just like any other international flight, although there were fewer women on board and the in-flight entertainment included an Indian movie.

Bollywood, the film industry based in Mumbai, makes two and a half times as many films as Hollywood, producing over 300 films a year. People in India, unlike most Western countries, go to a film for the complete experience, to laugh, to cry, to have their heartstrings pulled, to hear the music and watch the dancing, all in one movie and, if possible, all at one time. It does not matter that the dance scene in one frame has a backdrop of Switzerland and in another an island paradise. What matters is that the movie has a bit of everything: heavily romantic, a western mixed with a thug movie or a murder with a comic twist. The audience wants to lose themselves in another world and to forget about their own.

Udaan was 120 minutes of culture shock and unique in my film-going experience. The father of the heroine was killed in the first two minutes. Varsha, the heroine, because she was so beautiful, smart, sang well and had lots of money, was the target of the bad guys. They wanted her money and anything else they could get, so they employed a mad doctor at an asylum for this assignment. It was his job to ensure that Varsha would be rendered insane, by the application of serious monster electrodes, and preferably before the week was up. The setting was convenient, as the place was full of beautiful girls who could sing and dance. While the doctor rolled his big eyes and stroked his long mustache, among other things, squads of lovely women raced in and out, frenetically dancing the hoochy-coochy. As the heroine fought to escape the evil clutches of the doctor and his electronic brain-destroying machine, serious eye-bulging strangling took place. Throughout, the girls continued to frolic through what looked and sounded like a setting from *The Sound of Music*. Glancing away for a moment, I caught sight of two Indian businessmen on the other side of the plane. They were leaning forward, watching me watch the movie. I could see their smiles and guess at their laughter. I couldn't hear it, because of course the usual diabolical airline earphones were crammed halfway down my ears. They raised their glasses of whisky, the favourite drink of Indian men, nodded their heads, smiled and simultaneously mouthed the words, 'Welcome to India.'

Arriving at an airport in an unfamiliar country in the early hours of the morning always means trouble in some form or another. No matter how we try to guard against it, problems from an almost inevitable rip-off of some sort are almost guaranteed. New Delhi's Indira Gandhi International airport is dowdy. The lighting has the appearance of an emergency battery-operated service. All seemed well as we headed out through customs, where we noticed the State Bank of India was located inside the hall. Indian money cannot be taken into or out of India. It was 2 a.m. and we decided to buy some Indian currency for the taxi. *Namaskaar*, the in-flight magazine of Air India, suggested Thomas Cook or other professional exchange houses would offer the best rate of exchange, but this turned out to be incorrect: our credit card usually gave us a better deal.

It's true we could have managed the hotel better. Before leaving home I made some enquiries about accommodation for our arrival night. After receiving expensive quotes, I told the travel agent to forget it. 'We've been doing this for years. We can do it for half that. No, no don't book anything. We will fix it up when we arrive.' Travellers' memories are fickle:

they tend to remember the better experiences.

To get to a place like India you usually have to spend at least 24 hours travelling by plane. It doesn't matter which class you travel in: long spells of seat parking are involved. By the time we arrived all the blood in our bodies had settled in our backsides and our legs were pale, puffy logs of blood-drained uselessness. Our stomachs were bloated with the three, four, five meals we hadn't needed but ate anyway because we were bored. In a let-the-party-begin mood, we had a drink or two or three and, because we were dehydrated from the air-conditioning, the alcohol was retained longer and the short high was replaced by a long, gluggy low. It has taken me only 30 years of dogged repetition to figure this one out. No matter how experienced a traveller you are, arrival after a long flight, with two or three transfers, leaves you feeling dazed and exhausted. All your previously made promises to keep expenses reasonable are ignored and replaced with only two goals: a good bed and a hot shower.

Sure enough, there were airport touts all over the place who knew just what we wanted and were willing at any cost, entirely our own, to help us achieve our hearts' desire. The price of the room would turn out to be exorbitant and the quality poor. This, however, was impossible to tell until we were well out of screaming range of the 'authorised tourist agent' who took our substantial deposit.

I have never understood why, when you arrive at places like India or South America in the early hours of the morning, there are always thousands of people milling around the airport watching the new arrivals. Who are they? Why are they there? With our hotel deposit slip in our hand we were told to follow the driver, who led us out and through the crowds to the parking lot. Approaching the taxi ranks, we were informed that our man was not the driver but the guide who would take us to our driver. He demanded a tip. How on earth were we supposed to know how much it should have been? We didn't want to hurt his feelings. We just wanted to get to our nice quiet, clean room, for which we had just paid a deposit. We gave him a dollar and, sure enough, we insulted him. It was inevitable.

The taxi took off into the mist and the dark. There appeared

A Brush with India

to be a slight fog but it was actually the day's pollution steadily making its way down to the city floor. As we drove, we could see shacks up and down the road. Dim light illuminated paper walls and cast deep shadows on their occupants. It was supposed to be only 12 kilometres (7 miles) to the centre of town and our hotel but it took us 40 minutes to get there. When we finally arrived there were lots of smiles and a warm welcome. The taxi driver was happy, the porters were happy and the desk people were delighted. Everyone was thrilled to see us. The only question now was how many rupees it was going to take to keep from insulting them all.

We were tired and befuddled and although the sight of the large, sagging double bed instantly reminded us of other first night fiascoes, it seemed sleep would soon be possible. Turning on the light in the bathroom revealed corroding taps and a toilet that hadn't been cleaned since the Mogul Empire. 'We'll just have a shower in the morning when we can deal with the complications.'

What tangled beds we wove. This was our first encounter with the despicable single sheets and blankets on a double bed trick. It looks comfy but it is an illusion. At the first turn, the first wriggle, the bedding comes apart right down the middle, leaving bodies bare and sleep impossible. It is cold in Delhi at night in February. We tossed. We turned over and over. We were spooned bodies with one side constantly cold. 'Please God, it's 3 a.m., just allow me to sleep, this once.' It was no use. Gaston got up to check out the heater. He fiddled. He checked the plugs. Nothing could be coaxed into life. We rang room service. They could not be coaxed into life either. There was nothing left to do but take our clothes out of the suitcases and spread them over the bed.

After only four hours of sleep, we were sitting by the window staring down into the streets. New Delhi, Old Delhi, what did it all mean? Looking out from our fourth-floor room, everything looked so jammed together, so old, so chaotic. I was sure we had to be in Delhi, the old part of town. In front of my eyes was a city with the flimsy construction and composition of a pack of cards. It broke all the rules of perspective: walls did not lean like that and remain standing.

The British created 'New' Delhi in 1911. It was designed to

New Delhi

become the capital and political seat of the land the British called the jewel in the crown of their empire. As a carefully planned and constructed municipality near the site of Delhi, it instantly transformed the old city, which had been called Shahjehanabad in the times of the Mogul Empire when it was first built. It exploded with an influx of people from all over the Indian continent. Hope and two feet, long the strength of the Hindustani people, brought them to New Delhi in the anticipation of a fresh and better life. By the year 2000 the population had reached 13 million.

New Delhi houses an impressive collection of imperial sandstone government buildings, which are integrated with wide shaded avenues. This was the compound, the cosseted centre of British power; today it represents only a tiny outpost in a sea of newly poured concrete. It is a poignant reminder that nothing lasts forever. As for the British, forever lasted another 35 years. In 1947 India became an independent nation. At midnight on 14 August the land and the people became self-governing at last. After centuries of suppression by a multitude of oppressors, the people of India were finally free to begin the search for their own identity.

Consider the magnitude of that quest. In September 1999, a baby was born. Its birth was entirely unnoticed, but the infant had the dubious honour of bringing the total population of India to one billion, one-sixth of the world's population. The landmass of India is one-third the size of the United States with four times the amount of people. Every two seconds another baby is born. Every year an additional 15 million come into the world needing food and education. In late 1999 the World Bank published a report called, *Wasting Away: The Crisis of Malnutrition in India*. It reported that 50 per cent of children under the age of four were malnourished, 30 per cent of newborns were 'significantly underweight' and 60 per cent of Indian women were anaemic. A full one-third of India's people live below the poverty line, which means thanking God for his overwhelming abundance in giving one meal a day of lentils and a few peas. One-third means 80 million more people than the entire population of the United States.

India has made considerable progress in the last 50 years. There are positive statistics: life expectancy has increased from 39 to 63 and women have an average of three babies instead of six. This is not the United States or Australia where one nation speaks one language. India has 15 official languages and at least 845 dialects. Half the adult population is illiterate. Urdu is read from right to left, Hindi is read from left to right. The Tamils of the south read up and down. Some dialects are written in symbols.

God exists but in many different equally demanding voices. India is one of the most intensely spiritual nations in the world. Eighty per cent are Hindu, 11 per cent Moslem. The remainder are Christian, Sikh, Catholic, Buddhist, Jain and Zoroastrian. The Hindu religion alone contains over 3 million deities, a god for every need imaginable.

Even the physical topography conspires to complicate the lives of India's inhabitants. Drenching downpours unleashed by monsoons and whipped up by the northern monoliths of the Himalayas dump tons of water with harrowing inequality. Rajasthan receives almost no rain at all and has to endure merciless heat while each year West Bengal is knee-deep in water. On 29 October 1999, Orissa in the north suffered a super-cyclone that swept away uncountable villages and drowned 25,000 people. Fifteen million residents were left with no homes, no food and no drinkable water. In the succeeding years this catastrophe has become an annual occurrence.

Living in the south of India means speaking a different language, practising a different religion and having a different skin colour from the north. These differences apply in any direction. Over 70 per cent of the population is rural. It is not difficult to understand how easy it might be for an unscrupulous politician to sway a huge, rural, largely illiterate population: 20 different political parties struggle to bring unity where there is overwhelming diversity. Fifty years of independence is a flea on the elephant of time.

After breakfast, we were informed that 'someone from the tourist office' was waiting for us in the lobby. We remembered a vague mention of needing train tickets at the airport. A well-dressed man introduced himself and said he would take us to the office to discuss arrangements.

This was our first real sight of Delhi traffic, a little taste of what lay ahead. Three million moving vehicles paralyze progress and add to the pollution. Blue flames spit out fumes faster than they can be displaced by clean air: New Delhi lies fourth on the list of most polluted cities and our noses quickly became congested with the effects of black carbon. Private cars, taxis, trucks, buses and thousands of bikes and motorised rickshaws fill every available lane. Delhi's death toll from traffic-related accidents is higher than all of the major cities in India combined; five people die every day.

Sprawled across the road, relaxing in the right-turn lane of a frantic intersection, was a great horned, brown Brahma bull. As the sun's rays began to warm his back, he twitched with pleasure and went on with his morning ablutions. Approximately 40,000 cows wander the streets of New Delhi. The city has employed 100 cowcatchers to remove sick, dying and stressed animals. They are taken to a cow hospital, a gosadan, on the outskirts of town – a retirement home for the sick and the elderly. Since the cow is a beloved and a sacred animal, people sometimes misinterpret the cowcatchers' motives and abuse them: 'Why don't you stop bothering that poor animal? Can't you see he's doing no harm?' The cows that roam the streets are mostly vagrants, street cows that have been turned out because they're too old or don't produce milk. They suffer from malnutrition and, worse, from that new-age menace, the plastic bag. Cows forage. Where there is no grass they scavenge through garbage. They devour plastic bags containing table scraps mixed with glass, electrical cord, metal and razor blades. They die terrible deaths. And since the Hindu religion does not believe in interfering with impending death, the anguish of ruptured stomachs and split intestines can be seen and heard for days.

Gray blanket-wrapped bundles were beginning to stir from their sidewalk bedrooms. People squatted, cleaning themselves with toothbrushes made from sticks and scraps of towels. Tiny, raised platforms held barbers already busy with bristly customers. The morning light appeared filtered, half strangled by the density of the pollution. Mothers, as they do everywhere at this time of the morning, were feeding their children: spoons were lifted to naked babies, pancake chapatis, neatly folded, were handed to their older siblings.

A Brush with India

Men squatted with their backs against the walls, their legs folded impossibly compactly while they had their morning wash. The streets were bustling with people who made the concrete their homes, the sun's rays their alarm clock and their neighbours their living walls.

We arrived at the tourist bureau. We did not realise that it was the tourist-bureau-for-the-new-and-vulnerable-to India, of which there must be thousands. Earlier, when we had arrived at the airport, we were asked if we needed anything else such as tour guides, gold, jewellery, an extra woman, rugs, tea, a shave, a newspaper, train reservations, an astronomical guide? Thank God we only mentioned something about travel.

'Ah. Yes. Train reservations. But we can go to the train station tomorrow,' we said, so competently.

'Oh sir, no worries, no worries. There will be someone coming at the hotel tomorrow to arrange these things for you.' If you are fully conversant with India, this is a great service. The only trouble is that 'fully conversant' and 'India' are incompatible phrases.

What can I say? We'd only had four hours sleep. Gaston had come to India to work, to paint, to bring back some of the glorious colours of the subcontinent. We thought we would just hop on a train, get off, paint something suitable and continue.

The travel agent behind the mahogany desk was dressed in a navy blue pinstripe suit, three-piece. The desk had a glass top that covered the seemingly hundreds of postcards from seemingly hundreds of fabulously happy former clients.

'Would you like English tea or chai?'

'Chai, please.'

We pretended sophistication, familiarity, though it was our first cup of Indian tea. Chai is a mixture of black tea, boiled up with milk and copious amounts of sugar. It also contains various spices such as cinnamon, cloves, cardamom, ginger and nutmeg. The word chai, which simply means tea, is the same in Arabic, Greek, Hindi, Russian, Turkish and Swahili. Chai is a sweet refuge in a cup.

We tried to explain what we wanted. His elbows rested on the desk, his hands were folded together and the numerous gold rings on his fingers looked recently buffed and polished.

New Delhi

Occasionally, he yelled in Hindi to the lackeys hovering near his room. His large brown eyes revealed little of how hard he was concentrating on getting the maximum amount of money out of us. 'I have the answer for you.' We thought he might.

We decided after a little consideration, somewhat blurred by our lack of sleep, to hire a private car and a driver for three weeks and drive through and around the state of Rajasthan. We would also purchase tickets from Agra to Varanasi and Varanasi back to New Delhi. We wanted to leave right away. As time was needed to arrange the train tickets we would pick them up in Agra at the end of our car hire.

'Does the driver speak English? What about the fuel? Are we responsible for the driver's meals and accommodation?'

'I can assure you that the gentleman speaks better English than I do,' he purred in pure public school English. 'Our company pays for all petrol, food and accommodation. You will never have to concern yourself with the driver's welfare. He will take you anywhere you want, any time of the day or night. In addition, our drivers are thoroughly conversant with the roads and conditions. We have only experienced men who have been driving for us for years. Should there be any problem, any problem whatsoever, you only have to give our office a call.' And he began writing on a glossy calling card the phone number of the office and 'my personal number', in case we should need him. We handed over the US$1200 for the 21 days for the car, our illustrious driver-guide and the four train tickets.

Outside the office we were introduced to our driver and shown the vehicle. The car was a Hindustani Ambassador, white, with curtains fitted over the rear window and the two side windows. Each had little ties that could be removed so they could be drawn back. I thought of E.M. Forster's *A Passage to India*, with its British memsahibs and their parasols, long white gloves and generous ropes of pearls. The Ambassador is the same model as the 1940–50 British Morris Oxford, a car made for men to tinker with, a larger, messier version of a Meccano set. Ambassadors will last forever if lavish, slavish love is continually applied to them. Mechanically, they have never changed. Every car maintenance shop in India is equipped with spare parts for the Ambassador car.

If you break down, several million people will know how to fix your vehicle. With 2000 kilometres (1200 miles) in front of us it seemed like a hedged bet.

Dinesh, our driver, was a handsome young man. He seemed quiet and reserved, but we put it down to his being shy and, after all, we were strangers to one another. Before we left New Delhi, we drove over to his house to pick up his suitcase. While we were there, we met his older brother and some other men who gathered around us in great excitement. They were so happy to meet us, so gallant and gracious. His brother repeated over and over how lucky we were to have Dinesh as our driver: 'Good boy. Very good boy.' They constantly shook our hands, his hand, each other's hands and fussily patted Dinesh on the back. He busied himself with little pieces of paper the men had given him, finally folding them carefully and putting them in his brown wallet. Lowering his eyes, he smiled at the men, put his suitcase in the back and at last we were ready to begin our journey to Rajasthan.

The Rajput princes controlled Rajasthan for over 1000 years. They were a noble race known for their honour, independence, great fighting abilities and pride. Rajasthan, the second largest state in India, achieved its current boundaries only by late 1956, almost 10 years after independence. This is a strategically vital area as its western boundaries are with Pakistan. The desert kingdoms and their princes and maharajahs took their time and were finally granted financial remuneration to ensure they would continue to live as they had done before. But it was not to last: in 1971 Indira Gandhi abolished all payments to the former rulers of India and today the title maharaja represents only respect and social status. Their former homes have been turned into sumptuous palace-hotels, sometimes the only means of income for a modern maharaja.

To the west is the great Thar Desert, also called the Desert of Death, which encompasses almost 70 per cent of the state of Rajasthan. Daytime temperatures vary from 22°C to 50°C (74°F to 120°F) or more. We were there in February, wintertime.

Of all the regions, Rajasthan encapsulates the essence of India. Jaisalmer is the quintessence of a desert fort, eternally strong and enduring, an ageless oasis for caravan traders and desert nomads, and nothing rivals Meherangarh Fort at Jodhpur,

New Delhi

where all the fantasies of harems and warfare and desert politics became reality. Pushkar is a living religious icon, special to the Hindu people. Jaipur is India today, alive, colourful and dynamic mayhem. All over Rajasthan the women are among the most beautiful in the world and the men with their turbans and swirling moustaches are defiantly dazzling.

Our first stop was to be Jhunjhunu, a small town in the Skekhawati region, 245 kilometres (150 miles) west of New Delhi. We were on the road for only an hour when we stopped at a local dhaba, or roadside restaurant to have our first lunch. The local menus were absolutely, completely unintelligible. We thought that the study of several guidebooks and a few nights at an Indian restaurant before we left might have helped, but the only two small oases in this desert of words were soup and naan bread. The tablecloth presented an interesting pattern of culinary statements from numerous previous diners, but we didn't let it interfere with our enjoyment of the fine vegetable soup and potato-stuffed naan bread.

The main highway leading west out of Delhi was four-laned, straight and travelled through an industrial area. It wasn't long, only minutes after we had lunch, until we branched off toward Skekhawati, on what started as a two-lane road. We hadn't realised what a thing of absolute bliss a highway was until the surface began to disintegrate. I didn't dare look at Gaston. I knew he hated rough roads. Those amazingly contaminating blobs of oilpaint were doing their best to jump out of their metal jails. A minefield of potholes stretched out endlessly in front of us. We drove slower and slower. For me, the surroundings were so breathtaking that the bounce of a pothole merely turned my head in another direction towards another amazing sight.

Slender women with enormous bundles of sticks balanced on their heads walked down the road in groups of three or four. It didn't take long to make the connection to the hundreds of mangled trees that lined the road. February is the last month of winter and I wondered how these trees would survive the merciless summer heat without their branches and new leaves. When I asked Dinesh what the trees were called, he replied, 'Dead trees.' We were just getting to know one another so I wasn't sure whether to laugh or just settle for his deadpan expression.

19

It was a Friday and, according to our driver, an auspicious day for weddings. The giant tent structures, called shamianas, which covered wedding parties were sometimes as big as whole streets, gardens glowing with twinkling lights. We saw other Ambassador cars decorated like Christmas trees in diamond patterns of silvery tinsel. We discovered another talent of this vehicle: it can hold an infinite number of people. At first, seeing six or seven faces behind the front windshield was eye-catching, to say the least. In the back of the wedding car, also with five or six heads bobbing up and down over the potholes, was the object of the big event, the bridegroom, being ferried around from house to house until wedding time. You could always tell which one he was – the small, terror-stricken, unsmiling one in the middle.

Along the roadside were enormous fields of mustard. The scenery constantly switched from comic to tragic, from coarse to delicate. The tips of mustard plants swayed in the breeze like golden butterflies in a nest of emerald green feathers. Dinesh told me the oil of the mustard plant is excellent for headaches and massaging.

Their dress and their diminutiveness makes the women of Rajasthan seem like maharanis, princesses from the days of the rajahs and the Rajputs. Out in the desert, the colours of their saris are shockingly intense. Their tiny bodies are covered in brilliant pink, dazzling orange or azure blue; they wear gold at their neck and wrists. Some walk in the half-light of the dust and the evening sun with large bowls of green grass perched steadily on their heads. From a lifetime of carrying objects in this way their posture is that of a model on a catwalk. The statistics about the women of Rajasthan, about their rights or their extreme lack of them, do not make easy reading: women are not allowed to own property; their standard of education is abysmal; the stories of new wives being 'accidentally' burned to death are frightening. And although there are dozens of groups fighting to rectify these gross injustices, progress is painfully slow. But they look so beautiful in their colourful saris. They give such joy to the eye, when there is often nothing to be seen but poverty and relentless desert.

Along the road were more dhabas. Neem trees shaded

wooden porches and charpoi, string beds, were laid out for men to have a sleep as they paused in their journeys. Pigs and piglets, goats and dogs lounged in the outer periphery of the restaurants, constantly looking for scraps of food. Puppies lay dead along the road, the lowest in the food chain and the most reckless. Large crowds of men gathered in tight circles playing cards. Dinesh told me they didn't play for money, only for fun. It sounded like more dead trees to me.

It was starting to get dark and we were exhausted from lack of sleep and the relentless jarring of the road, which had now deteriorated to a single lane. Gaston hardly spoke. 'At this rate,' I thought, 'he's never going to be relaxed enough to even think about doing a painting.' This was day one and although I was having a great time just looking out the windows, I did begin to wonder how things were going to work out for him.

Chapter 2

Shekhawati to Bikaner

It was difficult to make clear to Dinesh why we were in India and what it was we were looking for. If he had understood it from the beginning, we probably would not have wound up in Jhunjhunu or Mandawa. He thought we were like other tourists who came to the Shekhawati region to see the famous painted havelis.

Shekhawati is a delicious mouthful of a word. It means the garden of Shekha and comes from the name Rao Shekha, a 15th-century chieftain. One of the major ports south of what is now called Rajasthan is in the state of Gujarat. To deliver goods north to Delhi and the northern areas, traders had to pass through Shekhawati. The astute chiefs living in the area made sure the levies imposed for travel through their land were more favorable than those of their neighbors, so in time the towns became important trading posts and the chieftains skilled traders. By the late 19th-century they had become experienced enough to realise that, in order to make even more money, they would have to conduct their affairs in seaport cities like Bombay and Calcutta, where the British were opening up large ports. Instead of taking their families with them they went alone and returned periodically. As they became increasingly wealthy, they built bigger houses and the tradition of painted havelis or houses developed. The more wealthy the merchant the more elaborate the designs of the paintings which took the form of murals or frescoes on the walls of their houses, inside and out. Now, as well as being decorative, they are historic and informative mirrors of history. At first, only flowers and designs were used, but no human or animal forms. Later, however, they became elaborate scenes of the Rajputs' royal courts. Just before the decline of the painted haveli, Western images became popular with murals of ships and, particularly charming, trains filled with foreigners in strange clothing.

The great tragedy is that these marvellous examples of architecture with their outstanding frescoes are fading and may one day soon disappear forever. Many buildings are in a poor state of repair and it seems inevitable that, little by little, the desert winds will erase their existence. Some houses have beautiful interiors where the families are attempting to renew the frescoes but most are disintegrating. Many of the former merchants have gone on to become the most outstanding businessmen in India, but their former homeland is now one of the poorest parts of the country. Complicated family disputes and government land reforms have also claimed large areas.

After a bumpy nine-hour ride in the car we arrived in Jhunjhunu, tired and hungry. We were relying on Dinesh to take us to reasonable and safe accommodation but after consulting his scraps of paper he couldn't find the hotel he was looking for. We never make advance bookings because we never know how long we are going to stay: it could be hours or it could be a week, depending on what Gaston finds to paint. We explained to Dinesh that we wanted medium-priced hotels.

The streets looked eerie. The lighting was almost non-existent and sand rose in clouds, falling with the meandering wind. People and animals wandered the streets looking as if they, too, were looking for a place to rest. Down a dark road we saw a sign, Hotel Jamuna, so we pulled in. We could just make out the forms of buildings, some of which had conical thatched roofs. A large fire was burning on the ground, startlingly red in the black night. Gaston went off to see if there was a room available for the night. 'We're in luck. They have one room left. It's the honeymoon suite.'

After the accommodation in New Delhi, I wondered what this room was going to look like. In the intense darkness we walked down a short road to a stucco building; our room was the end one on the ground floor. If this place was full of other customers, they were amazingly quiet. The heavy padlock was removed from the door, the lights were turned on and we stepped straight into... show time! All the walls and the ceiling were covered with vibrant and intricately detailed paintings of flowers and women, interspersed with squares

A Brush with India

and circles, cleverly integrating mirrors. The attendant smiled, lifted his eyebrows and looked at Gaston. Then he put on the electric heater. I caught the slow grin on Gaston's face.

Dinner was under the thatched hut. It was cold inside and I felt glad to have brought a coat. The open fire was outside the dining room door and next to it a red-turbaned man was playing a stringed instrument. The high-pitched music floated in the air, plaintive, sensuous and strange to our ears. The floor of the dining room was compacted dried cow dung, efficient and odourless. Around the room stood tables and chairs and other lower tables with couches and big cushions. We were the only customers. The tall waiter, who wore a high-collared Nehru jacket and loose pajama trousers, seemed unfriendly. We looked at the menu, but comprehension was nil. 'Tomorrow,' I promised myself, 'I'm going to write down menu translations.' At the waiter's suggestion we ordered curried eggs and fried tomatoes and ate them in the semi-dark. I felt uneasy, unsure if we had committed some gross tourist transgression, though I couldn't think what it might be. I watched carefully as an Indian couple came in. They sat on the low couches, ate peanuts and ordered a drink. She wore a gold ring in her left nostril, a red dot on her forehead and part of her sari over her head. She never spoke. A well-brought-up Indian wife still never speaks in the presence of her husband if other people are present. When she marries she becomes nameless. For example, she will be known as Mr Goopal's wife and later, if she has a son, as the mother of Mumal.

Jhunjhunu is close to the small village of Deorala where, in 1987, an incident took place that created world news. An 18-year-old married woman by the name of Roop Kanwar supposedly committed sati or suttee. When her husband died she threw herself into his funeral pyre in an act of religious, and traditional belief.

The Indian people are extremely pragmatic. Just when you are absolutely sure you understand a situation, another explanation comes along that completely transforms the original conception and leaves you floundering about your original thought. The Indian capacity to understand and accept multiple explanations as normal is a constant revelation.

The story of Roop Kanwar is an example of multiple

explanations and complex clashes of modern life and old customs. The story goes Roop committed sati upon the death of her husband and she did this by her own free will. Those who were against it were sharply reminded by the young girl that they themselves would be cursed forever if they tried to prevent her. Because every person knew what was going to happen by the time the funeral cortège arrived at the pyre of her husband. A policeman arrived during the cremation but it was too late to stop the apparent suicide.

Sati or suttee – the word comes from Sanscrit and means chaste or devoted wife – is an old custom, described and practised by the ancient Scythians and Thracians. In India, for hundreds of years, it prevailed as a custom to confirm the idea of an everlasting marriage and was even made a law by some tribes. A wife would not dare poison her husband, as his death would mean she would have to join him on the funeral pyre. The concept was that a woman must remain faithful to her husband even after death and, in the old Rajasthan regime, there were hard consequences for a widow who decided not to commit sati. She was not allowed to remarry. The Hindu religion said that if a wife did not join her husband immediately by committing suicide, then she would join him in the afterlife following her death. If she remarried, how could she join two husbands? (It didn't seem to matter that he was likely to have had any number of wives in his lifetime.) If she refused to commit sati she was required to shave her head and live in the care of and by the generosity of her children. If they could not take care of her she was thrown out into the street. The rest of her existence was to be spent in pious, nun-like humility, giving and accepting charity. There was no release until death took her to her husband. On the other hand, a woman who committed sati was considered a saint, and the place where she died was revered as a holy site.

How can we accept the logic of sati or of jauhar, an old Rajasthan custom where wives committed suicide when news of their husband's death in battle was imminent? There are many historical records of the victors of war entering a Rajput city to find the entire population dead. Rather than face dishonour at the hands of the enemy, the women had burned themselves and their children to death.

A Brush with India

Abu-ul-fath Jalal-ud-din Muhammad Akbar, born in 1542 and India's greatest Mogul emperor, understood that sati was neither logical nor humane and took the first steps to abolish it. A man of the people, he listened impartially to everyone, made himself available and initiated great humanitarian reforms. He is quoted as saying, 'It is a strange commentary on the magnanimity of men that they should seek their deliverance through the self-sacrifice of their women.' But tradition dies hard: after his death, sati was reinstated. It was not until 1829, nearly 225 years after Akbar's death, that the British finally made sati a punishable crime.

The police stated that Roop did not die of her own free will. They had witnesses who swore she was drugged with opium and placed on the pyre with her dead husband's head in her lap. The flames roused her but when she tried to escape she was forced back and the chanting of the local villagers drowned out her screams. The witnesses said the villagers were capable of doing such a terrible thing because they believed they would 'benefit spiritually'.

The police had other reasons to believe it was a murder. When a voluntary act of sati has been committed, within a short time a shrine is set up as a memorial to the woman and her 'holy act'. Certain castes, like Rajputs and Brahmins and banias (a merchant caste) benefit commercially as thousands of people make pilgrimages to the place of death. They pray. They give donations. They need accommodation and food. There is money to be made. The testimony of the dead man's family did not completely ring true either. Crucially, as in other recent deaths of sati, Roop's parents were not informed of their son-in-law's death. Had they known, they would certainly have come to their daughter's side and not permitted her to die.

Twelve days after the death of a woman who commits sati, a special ceremony called the chunari is held. At this time, a red scarf is placed over a trident, which marks the grave. A week before this ceremony, in Roop's village, nearly 10,000 people came each day to touch the spot where she died. With the pilgrims came the new shops and makeshift stalls selling everything this enormous influx of people might need, including souvenirs. Among the memorabilia were fake photos showing the devoted wife smiling, sitting upright and cradling the head of her dead husband while she waited for the flames to consume her.

It is impossible to say exactly what happened at Deorala. Although it is against the law to commit sati, the government was reluctant to stop the ceremony. The villagers say that, because of the media coverage, they are now known as wife burners. The sacred spot of Roop's death is guarded by the military and no photos are allowed. The people of her world are unlikely to say this was a crime. They are more likely to say, 'A long time ago this custom was a law. People have the right to make their own decisions. If a woman accepts the faith of her society and wishes to make this sacrifice, who is there to say she is wrong?' The 'who' applies especially to people who do not believe in or understand the conviction of a particular religion. Only time and education can change the customs of so vast a population.

Walking back to our room on our second night in India, I began to wonder about the role of women in Rajasthan. I looked at the walls and ceiling of our bedroom with its paintings of women in beautiful clothing surrounded by flowers and birds. I remembered the woman in the dining room, how modest she was. Should I take it as a sign of her secondary position or was she just feeling quiet that night? Who painted the women on our walls and ceiling, and why? Were they intended to glorify women or only to stimulate the bridegroom? Nothing is ever straightforward in India. A strong reason for visiting the country is that the opportunity for contemplation becomes a normal part of every day.

I have often been the subject of my husband's paintings and many of them have been nudes. People are inquisitive about this. I never think of them as paintings of myself: I am just a subject like a still life or a landscape. The real importance is how well the artist captures the colour and warmth of the skin, the essence not of one but of all women. Who buys these paintings? The answer, in the overwhelming majority, is women. Women think of a nude painting as representing all women; men think of it as portraying a particular woman.

The next morning we were on our way again but not before having breakfast in the strange dining room. The tall waiter was all smiles. We couldn't understand his change of behaviour, but we smiled back. He told us how he had worked at the rajah's palace in Mandawa for 17 years. It is now a hotel for foreign tourists. In the daylight we saw that the cow dung walls had pieces of glass, shells and mirrors imbedded in them in little shapes and patterns of birds and flowers.

One of the most difficult things for women when travelling in a private car in India is to find a suitable toilet. Later I learned to keep my coffee or tea consumption to an absolute minimum if we were travelling. Initially, I naively thought I was going to find a toilet at a petrol station or next to a courthouse or in a public garden. Later in the day, unable to wait any longer, I made a plea to find a toilet. For Dinesh that meant, 'Stop the car!' He pointed to a long brick wall in the middle of the town we were passing through: it was the local latrine. Necessity dictated that I would just have to get on with it but I hurried as much as possible because I didn't want the local populace lining up to have a peek at how the 'phoren' did it. Because I was wearing a straight, ankle-length skirt with a slit up to the knee on one side, no matter how I crouched there was still a lot of dimpled pink flesh showing. Remembering the full skirts of the local woman, I thought about them in quite a new light. I crouched. Gaston yelled, 'Further, further.' I hauled my skirt down and moved a few yards down the wall. No matter how far I kept moving, he kept yelling, 'Further, further.' When I got back into the car, Gaston and Dinesh seemed rather sullen. I had the feeling they thought I had not handled the situation very well. How easy for men to say.

The road to Mandawa was just as bad as yesterday's had been. The jarring, rib-crunching potholes went on and on for endless miles. But the redeeming feature, once again, was the endlessly astounding sights around us. There has to be, in the *Guinness Book of Records*, listings of how many people you can get into a bus, a car or a rolling vehicle – and all those records must have occurred in India. In front of us a bus would appear, with 150 people on it, and in it, balancing on any appendage and teetering on top. Worst of all, the buses seemed to have slightly flat tyres on one side so they leaned dangerously towards our car. When the passengers saw us in our smart white Ambassador, they all waved to get our attention. At first I waved back but quickly realised that several dozen passengers might actually come to serious grief trying to wave in return. There were also strange three-wheeled cars that looked like something out of a science-fiction movie – moving balls of body parts. If we dared to look, everyone smiled, handkerchiefs fluttered, arms and legs bounced and waved as if seeing us was somehow making them frantically happy.

We passed rows of children carrying shiny tiffin pails, which contained their lunch. In a place where great swirls and clouds of dust and sand reign supreme and where water is scarce, the schoolchildren we saw were spotlessly clean and scrubbed. The girls, especially, looked extraordinarily pristine. Their long tunics were pale blue and the loose-fitting trousers white. To complete the outfit a white scarf was either slung back over each shoulder or draped softly over their heads. When I asked about the schooling in Rajasthan I learned that only 5 per cent of Moslem children attend school and they are boys only: no girls are allowed and the boys are educated for only five years. All Hindu children attend school. Boys can attend free for the first eight years but the girls attend free for twelve years. School starts at ten in the morning and finishes at four, from Monday to Sunday.

I felt confused by this information, as I knew Rajasthan had the second lowest literacy rate in India: only 40 per cent of the people could read and write. Breaking down the figures into a male/female ratio results in only a 21 per cent literacy rate for women. It didn't make sense but here was the walking proof that considerable numbers of children were on their way to school. It wasn't until much later that I discovered I had been told the truth, but that the person who told me was a Hindu. There was another truth I just hadn't thought about yet.

Mandawa was only 25 kilometres (15 miles) from Jhunjhunu but 100 years back in time. The asphalt had long disappeared, if there had ever been any. The main street was crowded with people and animals. Cart vendors sold fruit: bright oranges and stacks of bananas. The smell of hot peanuts and a curious white sweet candy swept past our noses. Blacksmiths and cobblers knelt in the dirt. The men wore various coloured

A Brush with India

turbans and the women hid their faces under semi-transparent shawls. Cows, buffaloes, pigs, dogs and camels all jostled for space. Into my mind came the famous scene from *Star Wars*, where Luke Skywalker and Chewbacca walk into an interplanetary bar and Luke says, 'The people in this place are really strange, man.' It didn't, however, take me more than a few minutes to realise, by the reactions of the people on the street, that if anybody was strange, man, it was us.

When our car stopped Dinesh warned us the town was full of pickpockets and to be very careful. 'Many cheaters!' was a phrase he reminded us of at every stop. Suddenly there was a flurry of little brown, dusty, faces. Arms and hands thrust themselves into the open car window. The cacophony of different languages was indecipherable, but the meaning was plain. We rolled up the windows while Dinesh displayed his most disapproving look. Against the closed windows a young beggar girl, who had unintentionally stabbed me with her fingernail, showed me her hand – one finger in particular – at the base, thick, yellow pus oozed down into her palm. My stomach did a flip-flop of repulsion, as much for the finger as the smile on the child's face.

It was not made exactly clear to us what we were doing here in Mandawa but Gaston knew there was a bank where we could cash some travellers' cheques. Still foolishly clinging to Western customs, I frantically hoped the bank might have a toilet. As instructed by Dinesh, our hands clutching our money belts, looking straight ahead and talking to no one, we were ushered into the State Bank of Bikaner and Jaipur. Forget *Stars Wars*, now we were part of *Indiana Jones and the Temple of Doom*. Antiquated wooden desks and piles of papers with big elastic bands crowded into each other. Ledgers lay in multitudinous layers. When had I last seen a ledger? A hierarchy of employees was visually apparent. This was particularly noticeable when the really big boss, big in many ways, arrived a little later. He, of course, had a room of his own: he had nothing to do with the rabbit-warren front office. His suit, sophisticated and chic, had to be Armani or Indian-Armani at the very least. Much low bowing and a tray of tea followed closely behind him. We, naturally, were forgotten. Not that it mattered – it was all so entertaining.

Shamelessly, I knew this was perhaps my only chance to visit a real toilet and I asked if there might be one. They were expecting my request; probably every woman tourist makes the same plea. Two large brass keys on a shining brass ring were brandished about like a birthday present and I was accompanied outside into an alleyway with two locked high fences at either end. A door was unbolted. With a sense of pride, I was shown the toilet. It was one of those Turkish numbers with a hole in the ground but it was clean and had the most beautiful, large door, which I could lock.

Back at the bank our travelers' cheques were still going through the banking process without the aid of computers. Our clerk was a stern, well-fed man who hardly had time to look at us. Hunched over his desk, he constantly busied himself writing everything down from ledger to ledger. We were brought tea. We waited. An hour passed; our bills were passed over to the man behind iron bars at the counter. It looked like we were getting somewhere. But no, he was the ledger reader who checked the ledgers and passed them back to the ledger writer. Eventually, we did get a handful of money, which looked like a pile of used and faded wrinkled crepe paper. Now, at last, we were free to do whatever it was we were here to do.

Painted havelis were the reason and before we knew it Dinesh introduced us to one of his 'brothers', who would be our guide. We trudged up and down through the dun-coloured sandy streets, gazing up at the hieroglyphics, trying to make sense of the frescoes on the wall. Most of the houses were locked and we could only peek through the gates. The houses were two or three storeys high with the rooms built around large central courtyards. The owners had long gone to greater homes at their seaport addresses. The tour of the havelis was not a great success. Gaston was becoming impatient and wanted to be on his way, with the potholed roads behind him. Dinesh had promised this would happen 'soon, soon'. Gaston's only concern was to find a subject that would give him the inspiration to paint. He also knew we were going to be asked for a tip and since we hadn't asked for this tour, a tiny thread of cynicism started to edge into his voice. Back at the car, it became either a trip or a tip, so I opted for the

A Brush with India

trip. Why is it all guides seemed to have a shop? I went alone and made it snappy: I bought one tablecloth and we were on our way.

Dinesh had been telling the truth: the road did improve once we got onto State Highway 11. It wasn't perfect but compared with the monster we had finally said goodbye to it was bliss.

Arriving in Fatehpur, we saw havelis which had been beautiful, but it was sad to see their murals so faded and chipped. The buildings were neglected, old and looked as though they would soon tumble into the streets, but Dinesh was determined we were going to see them. He drove into town and parked right in front of every building. He couldn't understand why we weren't racing out of the car. 'Photos? Photos?' was the puzzled question. It was impossible to get him to understand that we were looking for paintable not painted subjects. He just didn't get it. We were starting to get the idea that our special driver who spoke the Queen's English actually spoke very little. 'Yes, ma'am' and 'Yes, sir', plus a few odd sentences usually containing the word 'cheaters', came out at rare times. We were not really sure if he was just shy.

While trying to get out of Fatehpur, barging our way through the crowded streets, I noticed a tiny ply-box stall selling bracelets. Pink and blue, gold and green, every color imaginable, they were sold in sets of five. Little pearls on gold filigree sparkled in the sun. I got only a glimpse. It was a very popular stall with groups of veiled women crowding around in a frenzy of looking and buying. Naturally, I wanted to stop. I wanted to stop but I knew what would be forthcoming. 'Bracelets more important than glorious painted havelis, Ma'am?' And, 'Did you realise what time it was? And what about getting on a good road?' Once we were back to the main road, we began to see peacocks everywhere. They flew in front of the car and from one tree to the next, like enormous sparrows. We could hear them calling to each other like cats on amphetamines, a high-pitched loud meow. It was so odd to see so many peacocks, and in the desert as well. As the trees started to thin out I wondered where the birds got their water or food. Appropriately, the peacock is the national bird of India: proud, exotic and more than a little wild.

Now we were beginning to see more and more desert and less vegetation. What would happen to the road in a windstorm? I thought about the summer here, so incredibly hot and with so little shelter. Growing along the road were thorny khejri bushes that resembled barbed wire. They have a deep root system and are one of the few bushes able to survive in the desert. Locals collect them and use them as a barrier to keep animals out of living areas and cultivated fields. Khejri is sacred to some tribes and is sometimes used in marriage ceremonies. I hated the damn stuff. When I tried to hide myself for a quick road stop, the branches seemed to reach out and cling to anything they could get hold of. The prickles were an inch long, viciously curved with barbed hooks. Nomadic tribes with their sheep and goatherds were travelling along this highway in search of food. What food? Anything green is snipped off as high as a bullock head can reach, and then at camel height. Then, women come along and whack off the mangled branches for firewood. It is hard to believe it now but thick forests once grew in Rajasthan. Axes and overworked fields have done irreparable damage and the desert now claims fertile land inch by inch and turns it to dust. It reaches out and blots up every drop of water. This was only our third day in the desert and already we had small spots of blood in our noses from inhaling the sand and the dry air.

In the desolation of this uninterrupted desert there appeared structures that looked like temple domes. In the early evening, against a backdrop of a fading red-orange sun, four spired, domed columns rose in honor of God. They marked some of the old Persian wells, which were still working. It is understandable, in so parched a land, that temples were built at the site of water. Even within the safety of our car and with the promise of a hotel somewhere ahead, it was comforting to know they were there.

Bikaner, 500 years old, was once a major trading center on the ancient caravan route between central Asia and north India. As we arrived in this desert city of 500,000 people, our main concern was where we would spend the night. Our driver knew a place but even after frantically consulting his pieces of paper, which should have told him where to go and where presumably he had been, he still drove us round and round in circles. We made a complete circuit of Lal Garh Palace, an imposing red sandstone structure built 90 years ago. Bikaner is a flat town and Lal Garh rises out of the sand like a huge ornate pink castle. While we were trying to find our way we came across the Palace View Hotel. It was only a short walk from the Lal Garh and since Dinesh was not sure about 'his' hotel, we stopped to check it out. The hotel room was spotless, half the price of the previous night and the proprietors, Mr and Mrs Singh, were hospitable and understanding. Marirmale, the wife, wanted to know what we would like for dinner and understood that we might be missing some foods. I had read that the best food in India was home cooking and how right that was. This would be the only time we would see a woman working in a hotel and Marirmale was one of only two women I would be able to talk to during our entire journey. Only a small number of women in rural areas speak English confidently and in places like Rajasthan it is very unusual for a woman to work outside the home.

While we waited for dinner, we walked to the nearby palace, built by Maharaja Ganga Singh in memory of his father, Maharaja Lal Singh. Today, it is a ritzy hotel. If you only have two weeks in India and are charging through on one of those big, pushy tourist buses, it would be a memorable experience to live like a maharaja for a day or two. We pretended we were guests and had a look around – very Kipling indeed. When I first visited New Zealand with my mother in 1958, as tourists from California, I found British customs an intimidating challenge. Here in the middle of the desert the old English traditions were still socially obligatory. I smiled and winced when I saw the place settings for dinner with six pieces of silverware on both sides of the plate, and laughed at the memory of myself at 17, trying to figure out which piece was meant for what. Further down the hall was a smoking room to which I was sure the men might 'retire' for their port and cigars. Inside, we saw an interesting collection of paintings of animals: the artist's subject was the hunting and killing of tigers. More wincing. The walls were adorned with stuffed heads of beasts that once roamed in the jungles not far away. In other rooms we saw a billiard table, a library and a card table. Belgian chandeliers sparkled and swayed slightly in the evening air. Wandering outside, we marvelled at the intricate, delicate latticework of the red sandstone. It felt good to be out of the car and walking in the desert air. Surprisingly we saw Dinesh waiting for us at the main gate. He thought we needed our camera, which we left in the car, and had been patiently waiting for over an hour. We told him we would not be staying for more than one night, as we wanted to go on to Jaisalmer in the morning, and for some reason he seemed unhappy. I thought he might be unwell: he had been coughing quite a bit. When Dinesh nodded his head to mean yes, he moved his head from left to right instead of up and down. It seemed to say, 'If that's what you want, I will, but I'm not thrilled about it.' It wasn't until I saw others doing the same thing that I realised the gesture meant a simple yes, with no other connotation.

The Junagarh Fort, a formidable structure built in 1593 and encircled by a moat, and the Ganga Museum, with antique masterpieces of ancient civilisations, are among the interesting things to see at Bikaner. There is also the fascinating, government-managed Camel Research and Breeding Farm. Just like humans, at the age of five camels go to 'camel school'. It takes them about six months to learn basic commands such as kneel, sit, stand and left and right. When they have mastered these techniques they are ready to join the workforce. A pin is forced through their nose and reins are attached. Camels can eat about 20 kilos (45 pounds) of food and drink a colossal 90 litres of water each day. In summer they can work for up to a week without water, in winter a month. There are three types of camels at the school. From Bikaner there are the long-haired types with hair in their ears, known for their tremendous strength. The dark-haired female camels from Gujarat produce more milk than other varieties. And the third variety are the light-haired camels from the Jaisalmer area, famous for their speed. The breeding farm tries to produce a camel with the best attributes of all three varieties.

There is a unique temple, 30 kilometres (19 miles) south on the Jodhpur road, called Karni Mata. Although it has beautifully carved silver gates, most people come to see the rats, which have invaded the inner temple. Rats are a good example of the Indian attitude toward living creatures: total tolerance and respect for all life. In this temple it is best not only to walk carefully, because of the multitude of rodents, but also to shuffle your feet to avoid squashing their fat furry bodies. It is considered poor etiquette to wear shoes in a holy place, so it is necessary to walk through the temple barefoot. The rats are fed on grain and honey and looked after with great respect. In the eyes of the priests, stepping on a rat means killing one of the priest's ancestors.

Back at the hotel, chicken soup and chicken curry with various vegetables made a splendid change for dinner. Our hosts were generous and friendly and, after two days of pothole purgatory, we finally started to relax. We were now 456 kilometres (278 miles) west of Delhi and feeling far, far from home.

The next morning I had time to talk with the owner, Vikrau Singh. Until then we had really had little opportunity to talk with anyone. Many people speak at least some English, which is the official second language of India, and Mr Singh spoke perfectly with a very cultured accent. As we talked he became the first of many to tell us that politics in this country was in a very bad way.

'All politicians are corrupt and greedy and once they are elected will do anything to stay in government – even change parties! As we speak, crooked politicians are being brought to trial in a "special" courtroom, not the courtroom of the common criminal. No matter the outcome of the trial, they receive suspended sentences and never really spend time in jail. They, as a matter of assumed right, give all the perks and good jobs to their friends and family who become impossible to get rid of.' He went on to say if things do not change that there would eventually be a civil war. In a few weeks there would be a general election. He was hoping for a change.

England acquired India not with 5 shillings but because of it. The Dutch who were controlling the spice trade in 1599 raised the price of a pound of pepper and, by doing so, incensed the merchants of London, who banded together and formed the East India Trading Company. Formally sanctioned by Queen Elizabeth I, the company was given exclusive trading rights for all countries beyond the Cape of Good Hope for 15 years.

The first little galleon, the *Hector*, under the command of William Hawkins (yes, that really was his name), half captain, half pirate, arrived in India on 24 August 1600. Not really understanding the megalopolis he was going to find, he made his arduous way to the capital, which was then Agra. He was given permission to enter the compound and palace of the world's richest and most formidable ruler, Emperor Jehangir, the last of the great Mogul rulers. The omnipotent king was delighted with the Englishman's company and, incredibly, made him a member of the royal household. And as a welcome gift, Captain Hawkins was given the most beautiful girl in the harem, an Armenian Christian.

Soon afterwards, the emperor signed a document that allowed the East India Trading Company to have depots north of Bombay. This momentous decision changed the life and destiny of both India and England forever. The success of the venture was overwhelming. In the beginning, the English had no intention of taking territory: all they wanted was trade – spices of all kind, sugar, and fine silks and muslin cotton. Over the next 150 years negotiations were fairly amiable, but when disagreements occurred it meant the British company officers had to intervene in local squabbles. As a result, they became more and more enmeshed with local politics. Gradually, almost by default, they began to reverse their initial policy and pursue territory, though they never expected to retain their acquisitions. Inadvertently, they became, in time, the successors of the Mogul emperors. Paradoxically the Moguls and the British Raj lasted about the same length of time, the Moguls from 1526 to 1707 and the English from 1750 to 1947. By 1857 the responsibility for and destiny of a sixth of the world's population was held in the hands of a 38-year-old woman, Queen Victoria.

The British were not interested in assimilation. Everything was imported from England: if they could have brought Brighton Beach on a boat, they would have. They lived apart. They imported their legal system, their schools, and their business and administration systems. And, possibly most important of all, they brought the English language: anyone who wanted to deal with the British was going to have to speak English. They brought all their social customs. They had

A Brush with India

grand imperial balls in the Himalayan mountains. They went to dinner in black ties at a 'suitable table' in the middle of the jungle. They taught their Indian servants to cook roast dinners and game pies and plum puddings. Cricket, the beloved game of the English, later became the obsession of the Indians. Golf was introduced 30 years before it reached New York. Procedure and etiquette were everything, but social exchange between Indians and the British was nonexistent. The British set themselves apart as absolute and paternalistic rulers, as a superior race. They left in 1947 only because they ran out of money and men: the two world wars in the first half of the century killed too many young British soldiers, the British economy was devastated and India was wild with impatience to be free. Gandhi and Viscount Mountbatten led the way.

I asked Vikram Singh how he felt about Britain's heavy influence on his country – did he perhaps resent it? Even out here in the desert from time to time we saw signs that said 'Be proud, be Indian, buy Indian'.

He replied, 'Before the British came we were not united, we were a discordant land and many different people with no organisation. We have been pillaged and conquered throughout our history. The British came and put organisation into our lives. Now, they have gone and we are free.' He looked straight into my eyes, as Indian people do when talking, and I could see the great love, expectation and impatience he had for his nation.

We had 335 kilometres (200 miles) to drive to Jaisalmer, the city that we had dreamed of for many months. It would be a long drive. Our little Ambassador car did not seem able to go faster than 70 kilometres (42 miles) per hour. When we left early in the morning after a big English breakfast our account, for dinner, bed and breakfast, was very reasonable. We felt sorry to leave Marirmale and Vikram and their two girls and would have good cause to think of them over the next month. The clean room and the good food were a combination we would never have again.

We took off in the usual cloud of dust and were on our way. About 100 kilometres (60 miles) down the road we made a stop in the middle of nowhere – there were no trees, buildings, nothing but endless desert – because Dinesh wanted to check the oil pressure. February is winter in the desert. It was a rather balmy 27°C (84°F) and there was just a gentle breeze. I stayed in the car while he and Gaston got out to see what was happening under the hood. Within three or four minutes, where there had been only sand as far as the eye could see, a young girl appeared. Where had she come from? It was difficult to guess her age but I would estimate 12 years old at the most. It appeared she was married as she wore a large red bindi on her forehead. She came to the open window and made a sign, pointing with one finger to the palm of the other hand and saying, 'Peen, peen.' (It had taken me some time to figure out this meant pen, as in ballpoint pen or a pencil) What would she or the other dozens of other children, who previously had asked me for a 'peen', do with it? Perhaps it was some sort of status symbol: 'See what I got from the tourist'. Or maybe they could use it if they were lucky enough to go to school. I wish someone had told me before I left to take a truckload of peens. She was pretty and delicate, her eyes clear and her teeth white. She soon forgot about asking me for a peen. Our only common language, grins and curiosity. We studied each other as if encountering a new species. Her dress had once had a green and gold floral pattern. Now it was badly faded and had a large tear on the shoulder and another at the hem, so that it slipped off her small shoulders. She didn't seem to mind when I took her photo. I wanted to give her something, anything, but I could only uselessly wave goodbye. No matter where we stopped, in this immense sandy, dusty emptiness, as barren as the moon, within minutes someone or something appeared. Even the Desert of Death is not a barren land.

We stopped at a restaurant at Pokoran, halfway to Jaisalmer, a huge place where tourist buses paused for lunch. We were uncertain about dining there because it had been our experience that such spots were usually the worst places to eat. But this time we were wrong. The menu was written in Hindi and English and the food was very good. I stuck to vegetables. I was getting used to a vegetarian diet: if you don't eat meat, nothing gets stuck in your teeth and although the food was spicy, I had less indigestion. Gaston had his first beer since we arrived in India. It was twice as big as he expected: beer is sold in 3/4-litre bottles in India. The notorious Kingfisher beer would sometimes be as clear as an alpine stream and at other times like a cloudy soup. Sometimes it was delicious and sometimes it tasted as if it was brewed in a rusty tin. How, Gaston wondered, could one possibly be so easy-going about something as sacrosanct as beer? But we laughed every time we ordered it, as across the top of the bottle in big capital letters was the charming expression, 'MOST REFRESHINGLY CHILLED'.

We were still some distance from Jaisalmer and didn't know what we would find once we got there. So far, it hadn't been great for painting. We were weary from the travelling and the dust and were still encountering a few potholes. We started to notice a change in the traffic: now there were huge trucks on the road, most of them severely overloaded. Dinesh told me he hated the desert.

Chapter 3

Jaisalmer

THE DESERT SEEMED ENDLESS, then slowly, a gigantic sand-stone castle appeared – enormous, striking, an overwhelming sight in the soft golden light of the afternoon sun. Jaisalmer is outstandingly beautiful, at once a welcome sign of shelter and food, and also redolent of great mystery and intrigue. Nothing in India is like Jaisalmer Fort: surrounded by enormous stonewalls and bulwarks, it stands alone in its isolation and grandness. Below the fort, on the desert plain, stood houses, shops and hotels.

We had travelled 1000 kilometres (600 miles) from New Delhi to get to the Golden City, as it is known, and had taken no account of when we would arrive, other than to make sure it was winter. We knew there was a desert camel fair at the end of January and, by chance, discovered that it was to begin the next day. Where were we going to sleep? Local tribespeople and foreign visitors alike had overwhelmed the little town of 45,000 people.

We looked at a few hotels but they were abysmal after our wonderful room in Bikaner. After parking, moving, going upstairs, downstairs and repeating the process several more times, we gave in and tried to find accommodation at one of the more expensive hotels. We drove out to Gorbandh Palace and parked alongside the herds of white tourist buses. Dinesh was unhappy and kept mumbling, 'Many rupees, many rupees.'

Why do I always feel as if I can't breathe when I get into one of these places? A doorman dressed like an Arab opened the door for me and I found myself in the middle of a large chrome and glass reception area. It was crowded. Oh, yes, as I had expected, they were here, the drawlers and the darlings. 'Could you posss-ab-lee get me …. darling?' Or, 'Darling, did you see that gorgeous little di-ah-mond?' And 'That wud be mah-vel-lous'. And, of course, 'Did you see those a-dorable abo-rigines on those little darling camels?'

Feeling totally intimidated but determined I went to the reservation desk to find the hotel clerk dressed in clothing suitable for the Arabian Nights. Wasn't I in India? I was embarrassed. He wasn't. I had to wait while he called Mrs Astor-Hilton over and gave her a fax. They had a nice little chat for several minutes. Since I had decided I didn't want to stay here anyway, I was not too disappointed when he told me, as if it were some sort of funny story, 'There are no rooms available, memsahib'.

Back we went to the Hotel Neeraj, just below the fort, the first place we had stopped. It was cheap and the staff were helpful and kind. According to our Lonely Planet guide it was 'clean, carpeted but otherwise unremarkable'. Two out of three is at least a majority. The double bed was no more than two hard planks with the thinnest mattress I had ever seen. The bottom sheets, of course, did not meet in the centre and we had to ask for two more, as there were no top sheets. On the walls were a few shelves, sticky and decorated with stains of old soda bottles. The carpet, of which the management was so proud, was wet a metre beyond the bathroom because the shower water ran straight onto the bathroom floor and out the door. We had no window – well, the window was in the bathroom. If we wanted a window, we could leave the bathroom door open.

The management was so proud of their hotel. 'It is very nice, yes? Very beautiful hotel. You like?'

The Indian smile, and the warmth that radiates from it, always made me like these people instantly. 'Of course! We love the hotel.'

We asked Dinesh to come back in two hours so we could get settled and have some rest. He gave us the usual disquieting head nod, but we were slowly getting used to it. He looked tired and I hoped he would have time to find a room and have some rest himself.

As we were getting ready to leave and have a look at Jaisalmer by car, we were accosted by the management, who kept insisting that our driver was, 'a good boy. This is a very good boy.' We knew this: he was very polite and drove confidently. He didn't take unnecessary chances on the road. He made a little temple out of the car each morning by

Jaisalmer

lighting incense and praying that everything would go well that day. He was a quiet, gentle person. I noticed his English improved greatly when it is just the two of us and he could take his time.

We felt anxious and excited to see the narrow streets and the Jain temple high in the fort. We received the now customary lecture about 'many cheaters' and were warned not to go with 'anyone, anywhere'. Normally, when we're looking for picturesque painting spots, I wait while Gaston investigates. It is no use for me to make suggestions: he has to find what inspires him. So now, while Gaston walked around, Dinesh and I followed him in the car. We started talking and I found out he was sick. In the two hours while we were resting he had tried to go to the local hospital, described in our travel book as, 'a nightmare. Dirty, crowded and often no running water with overworked staff'. They wouldn't see him because he didn't have a card for medical care. When he had finished driving us around, he was going to see a private doctor. Intruding on his privacy, I asked where he slept at night but he didn't want me to know. I could feel his reticence. 'There is a problem. The company does not give me enough money.'

Dinesh was paid 1000 rupees (US$27) per month and 120 rupees (US$3) a day while he was on the road. Did he sleep in the car? Our hotel was 500 rupees a day: how could anyone live on such a small sum? I never found out if he was telling me the exact truth. I believed he was. I did discover that the hotels where we stayed usually allowed Dinesh to stay too. His accommodation was either on the roof, or in a tent. Sometimes it was good and sometimes it wasn't and sometimes there wasn't any. Dinesh never complained, except this once: he was feeling desperate about being sick because he might not be able to drive the car.

In our room that evening, I felt overwhelmed by our overall personal ease in life. As we sped by, looking at this other world through the windows of our car, the gap between our lives seemed obscene. I felt remorseful that I thought our room was not good enough. Outside our wall there were men, women and children sleeping in the sand dunes. I was tired and also worried about Gaston. He had come here to paint. How was he going to find the courage? What would happen

A Brush with India

when he set his easel up in the street? Would he be mobbed? Would children stick their fingers in the paint, like they did in Morocco? The hard bed, the mosquitoes and the sound of voices, loud and plainly heard, made sleep elusive.

In the morning, as people do, we felt more positive. We discussed moving but, thinking we might make it more difficult for Dinesh, we decided to stay. He had found a doctor and was taking antibiotics. While we were eating our usual breakfast of toast and bright red, unidentifiable jam with watery coffee, the hotel manager came rushing into the dining room. 'You must see! Come, come. It is most beautiful sight. You never see anything like it again.'

It was the first day of the desert fair and people and processions were getting ready. Dozens of stunning riders on camels advanced toward us. Their animals, outfitted with multicoloured robes and heavy hand-tooled leather saddles, radiated aloofness, and superiority. These were the famous light-coloured camels from Jaisalmer, renowned for their speed – but not today. Right foot, long lope, left foot, long lope and pause. The sound of the soft chimes, the jingle of silver bells and jewellery around hooves and necks, the deliberate slow regard, the lashes so long that the eyes never look anything other than half open, the great height – this was the spectacle of the king of the desert. Attitude, attitude.

I could hardly wait for the fair to begin. This was better than the circus, better than Cinemascope, better than anything I had experienced before. These were real people at a real event with no sponsors and no commercials.

Dinesh arrived and suggested we go to the lake where the procession was going to start. Gadi Sagar Tank was originally built in the 14th century as a holding area for a water supply. Tilon ki Pol, the entranceway, is a sweeping, rose-coloured sandstone structure under an imposing gate. Legend says that a famous lady of the night offered to pay for the gateway to be built but the maharaja, Gadsi Singh, refused, saying it was beneath his dignity. It seems the poor raj would have to pass under it on his way to the lake, and couldn't bear the shame of having to walk beneath a gateway paid for by a prostitute. She outsmarted him by having it built while he was away, and by adding a religious shrine, a Krishna temple, on the

Jaisalmer

top. It was then impossible to tear down.

Strange, small temples and shrines stood in various places in the water. Though many tourists were strolling up and down the steps, it was a quiet place. Waterfowl swam noiselessly, making small ripples on the water. A young boy in poor clothing had been trying to sell me some small rock fossils since we arrived. He had probably got them from Akal, the fossil park, 14 kilometres from Jaisalmer. (Animal and plant fossils have recently been discovered there, indicating that the Thar Desert is a relatively recent phenomenon.) He followed me constantly, not obtrusively but inquisitively. We sat on the steps together and watched birds landing on the water. I tried to explain that neither Gaston nor I had any change. We didn't even have a 'peen'. He seemed so gentle. As I got in the car to leave, he smiled and put the little rock fossil in my hand: it was his present to me. I promised myself I would return and give him something. I never did, and the tiny rock lies accusingly at the bottom of my purse as a reminder.

Since there was no sign of the parade beginning, Dinesh dropped us off at the stadium where the fair was getting under way. Thousands of people milled around waiting to be seated. Rudely, the local people were brusquely pushed aside and told to wait while Indians of wealth and the foreign tourists were installed in the stands, the best seats.

Seated on the concrete steps in the full sun, we tried to stick it out but after half an hour, and with rapidly escalating heartbeats, we retreated to the top of the stand where there was a small area of shade. We could see it was reserved for dignitaries, as there were several enormous padded chairs with army personnel standing behind them. When the residents of the chairs finally arrived, we were told to go back down to the stand. In the pecking order it seemed we were number two of three: the first were the 15 padded chair residents, the second were us and the 500 other tourists, and the third were the 8000 locals. We watched with interest as the last group filed excitedly and in an orderly manner onto sheets and blankets spread over the sand. Directly behind the stadium, rising high on Trikurta Hill, stood the glorious, imposing backdrop of Jaisalmer Fort.

The proceedings began with a grand procession. First

came the camels and their riders, members of the Rajasthan Desert Patrol, and as they rode into the arena the whole stadium went wild with joy. The men looked resplendent in their saffron turbans and sashes, white tunics and pants. Each carried a long spear with a yellow and red flag. The camels accelerated in response to the cheers of the crowd. Following closely behind were the entrants for the Mumal and Mahendra lookalikes, the desert lovers. And finally the dancing girls arrived, hundreds of beautiful women and girls swirling and moving to the beat of desert drums. This time the crowd went berserk. The colours were extraordinary. Their saris, in shocking pinks, butter yellows, opulent oranges and fiery reds, were all worn with dazzling and ancient jewellery. The local Rabari women wore white bracelets from wrist to shoulder. Nose rings, earrings, toe rings and anklets, layers of gold, demure smiles and an elegant walk from a lifetime of carrying things on their heads made these women singularly splendid. We all rose and clapped, begging them to go around the stadium once again.

After we had finally settled down and the crowd became quiet, the first entertainment was the children's dance. Next came the native women and then the professional, traditional dancing women who moved in circles of 50, all colour, shimmer and grace. The sounds of drums, string and wind instruments wound their way into the mind like invading and potent incense. The women turned and swirled to show off their 14-metre skirts. Swinging ornaments and the sounds of hundreds of bells filled the air. The frenzy of the dancers was spellbinding, hypnotic.

It was too hot. We retreated once again to the shade high in the stand. This time, because we looked like classic heart attack candidates, they let us stay.

The first contest was turban tying and the local experts came up on stage. The turbans of Rajasthan are the most colourful in India. An integral part of a man's dress, they have many practical uses. Since they can be anything from 9 to 20 metres long, they can be used as a sheet to sleep on or a pillow. They identify which part of Rajasthan a man comes from, as well as his social class. They can be used to draw water from a well and, most important of all, they protect the head from the sun. Having tied turbans all their lives, the experts made it look easy. A wild flash of cotton and the cloth was wound expertly, tightly on their heads. The tourists were invited to try. Predictably, they were hopeless. Lining up on the stage, 12 contestants wound and turned the huge length of material into crumpled streams of flying, wilted, unwound failure. The crowd roared with laughter, loving every minute of it.

The next event was the Mr Desert competition, a beauty contest with a splendid difference: men, not women, vied to be the most handsome. Except for small changes in detail, their costumes were identical. The basic dress was a white tunic and dhoti – a piece of long white fabric drawn up between the legs, made to look like loose-fitting pants. On their heads they wore the hand-tied turbans of the Jaisalmer region, hand-painted in red, orange, green and purple, in a square and dotted design. On their feet, shoes called jootis, embroidered with oriental patterns of flowers and swirls. The toes were pointed and turned back. The insides of the shoes were lined in velvet; some had pearls, silver ribbon and garnets attached to the outside. On their backs, a length of coloured silk was tied, forming a wide ribbon that was arranged over the shoulder of their white tunic. Every man had a sexy moustache about 15 centimetres long, twisted into a long upward curl on both sides; the moustache signifies great honour. Their beards were so full they covered their entire necks. In their hands each man carried a heavy sword, a metre long, the sheath red, the hilt and tip gold. At their throats they wore heavy, ancient and elaborate silver jewellery. The tallest man was close to 2 metres tall and looked like he could grind a man to dust with a couple of fingers. Seen up close they looked intimidating and lascivious, two dozen Rudolph Valentinos. The movies could go to hell.

By the time the Mumal and Mahendra contest started it was late afternoon but there was not a restless soul in the stadium. There was once, long ago, a very handsome prince, Mahendra of Umarkot. He fell in love with Mumal, a princess of renowned beauty who came from Ludarwa. The first moment he saw her he knew he could not live without her. What to do? What to do? There were problems. First, Ludarwa was many hours camel ride from Umarkot. And the

A Brush with India

other wearisome snag was the eight wives Mahendra already had. The first problem was easily solved by Chekal, a camel of swiftness and daring, handsome and devoted, a camel prized above all other camels. After Mahendra had spent a few weeks sneaking over to Mumal's palace every night, the eight spouses felt there was a certain lack of enthusiasm in the royal bedroom. What to do? What to do? Get the camel, of course. As well as bludgeoning the camel nearly to death, they managed to make him lame for the rest of his life. Without Chekal, Mahendra was compelled to use another beast who was, well, to put it kindly, a dud. The very first night the camel got lost and it wasn't until early morning that the prince finally arrived at Ludarwa.

Now Mumal's sister Sumal had this habit of dressing up in men's clothing. Being sisters they liked to talk a lot and while waiting for Mahendra to arrive they gossiped long into the night and the early hours of the morning. When Mahendra finally arrived with his dopey dromedary, the two sisters had fallen fast asleep. Mahendra, not knowing about Sumal's cross-dressing habits, thought, as a man might, that his true love had found another. Broken-hearted, he returned to Umarkot. Mumal waited and waited but her lover never returned. She finally died of grief, as lovers will. Eventually Mahendra found out the truth and he, too, died from despair.

There are several variations of this story but the most important element is that it is a love story. Stories where people meet and fall in love, although opposed in Indian culture in marriage terms, are told with great tenderness and delight. The woman announcer pronounced the story of Mumal and Mahendra 'a love match for which the finest privilege is to suffer and to die.' This was the lead into the procession of Mumal and Mahendra lookalikes, a contest for children.

Tiny regal-looking girls perched high on camels, and dressed in royal red decorated with jewels and tassels, were led by young boys. They came two by two now, perfect little miniature Indian Romeos and Juliets. The most adorable contestants were a small Mumal and a tiny Mahendra, only three or four years old, dressed in white pantaloons and a red vest, and with a large painted moustache under his nose.

His sword was swung low on his body. He pulled the camel by its lead with great solemnity. As he approached the main stage he took out his sword, which had been dragging on the ground, and raised it high to the judges. The crowd loved the gallant effort. The procession made two more turns of the arena and the three finalists were chosen. Partially owing to the exuberance of the crowd, one more pass in front of the judges was called for, but by the time the last approach came the littlest Mahendra had had enough. In an act of defiance he strutted out on the stage, threw his turban down to the ground and, running to his father's arms, refused, absolutely, to return.

More music and dance performances were planned for the evening but a break of a few hours was welcomed. We walked back to our hotel in the warmth of the fading sun, and tried not to hold hands: touching one another in public is not considered polite in India. We felt tired but elated, happy we had made the effort to come so far.

In the evening we walked up into Jaisalmer. The city is a collection of ancient and crumbling buildings, which have slowly built up around the ramparts of the fort, there are fascinating little shops of all descriptions. Sometimes they are part of a building but they can also be cardboard shelters, or even large carts. There are no grocery stores as we know them in India: instead, even in large cities like Delhi or Agra, hundreds of tiny shopkeepers sell only a few items. Fruit and vegetables are sold exclusively on carts. Film, pens and paper can be found in small permanent locations. There were also a few places to buy alcohol. The brand names of beer were memorable: Golden Eagle, Knock Out, Guru, Rosy Pelican and, of course, our favourite, Kingfisher. The quality is not guaranteed. You pay your money and you take your chances.

Near the main entrance gate to Jaisalmer Fort, against the lower wall, was the smelly public toilet, which was for men only. It was so disgusting that the customers had a pee somewhere near the door, by the window or on the wall, but seldom in it. Ten steps away from the toilet was another 'shop', which had some very curious customers. I had a quick glance and saw that most were European. The clothes were Indian but

A Brush with India

the faces were plaster-white. What struck me most was their posture: they were lying down, lounging against the stone walls or standing with their eyes closed. The only clue was the word 'BHANG' hastily scrawled in crayon on a large piece of cardboard. Bhang contains either opium or marijuana and is mixed into a drink called thandai, a concoction made of poppy seeds, rose petals and herbs. It is most often consumed during the festival of Holi where people splash colours on each other to celebrate in a particularly joyous manner.

No one knows when opium was introduced to India. Medicinally it has been used for centuries but did not become a drug of habit until about 500 years ago. Certainly the East India Company encouraged its use by having farmers cultivate it, even to the detriment of other crops. In Rajasthan today, one in five households are affected by its use. It is socially accepted: opium is sometimes offered at Rajput ceremonies and weddings, and also at funerals. Occasionally, a host will offer opium water in the palm of his hand as a welcoming gesture. Long ago, when soldiers had to travel great distances, they were able to keep going because opium gave them a sense of euphoria and dissipated their fear in battle. In India today some workers demand poppy husks to be included as part of their wages, which suits the employers because productivity increases. India is one of the few places in the world where opium is grown legally: farmers grow it to supply the pharmaceutical industry locally and abroad. Birds often become addicted. Parrots love poppy seeds and once they have found a field of poppies, they stay forever.

We found a restaurant up several flights of stairs. The 'building' was made out of the thinnest of wood bulked up with layers of paper. The stairs were less than a metre wide, so narrow that we felt the impulse to turn one shoulder inwards to make sure we didn't bump into the walls. We passed the kitchen, a floor below the restaurant, and I resisted glancing in. Our table looked down onto an open square. There were no windows so it was easy to lean over the balcony and watch the street scene below: people meeting friends, tourists looking bug-eyed and lost, women in gorgeous saris, men in turbans, the odd camel, the cows, the children, the goats and the pigs. Gaston had a beer, and I had a banana lassi, a popular yoghurt

Jaisalmer

drink: both were 'most refreshingly chilled'. We ate some tasty chapatis. As usual, I ordered too many, but watching the cows in the street gave me an idea.

I had never paid much attention to the problem but now I wondered how these animals got enough to eat. In fact, there is a very good system. Each morning and again in the evening the daily household garbage is put out into the street. Sometimes neighbours combine their heaps of refuse. Cows, buffalo, goats, pigs, dogs, chickens and rats eat in order of size: the biggest first and the smallest last. They eat it all until there is nothing left but an abundance of blue plastic bags, which are then burnt.

The treatment of animals in India is a revelation. Cows are especially revered as a mother symbol and because they were considered a measure of wealth and a type of currency. Also, in times of drought the milk was sometimes the only source of food. Elephants, monkeys and birds all figure heavily in the stories of the Hindu, Jain and Buddhist religions, all of which believe that no harm should be done to any living thing. Cows, buffalo, bulls care not a jot if they are in the way of cars, trucks or people. I got used to leaning out of the window and hitting my hand on the car door to scare a cow off the road. Usually it just looked at me dully and, if we were in luck, would slowly meander off down the road at its own pace. They know they will never be harmed. Great bulls and huge buffalo walk around the street in the most nonchalant way. It is most odd to see how passive they are.

Curious to see how the bull in the square would react if I fed him some chapatis, I offered them to him, but quickly realised this was a mistake when he started to follow us around the city. I finally shook him off when it was getting dark. Now I was left with a pile of chapatis and ghee all over my hands, so when a buffalo caught my attention, I handed over the food, *tout de suite*. As I turned to go, I heard a whimper and looked down. A young dog was gazing me with a look so direct and needy that it was unnerving. With a further whimper and obviously in great pain, he raised his broken and bloody back leg for me to see. I had no food left.

Earlier that same evening I had another encounter with an animal as we walked home from the stadium. There was just

A Brush with India

enough light to make our way but a lot of dust stirred up by the big crowds. Glancing at some thorny bushes I noticed a dog. Again there was that curious sense of intense, visual contact. We kept on walking. Without warning, there was a rush of fur and warmth curling around my ankles. The same dog, his lips pulled back, his teeth bared, looked up at me in an urgent, pleading way. I couldn't get him out from under my feet and was frightened. What if he had rabies or some other disease? Before we could get him away, a man on a bicycle stopped and gently removed the dog back to the bushes. It all happened so quickly that I hardly had time to say anything. 'Thank you so much,' I called. 'Oh, it is quite all right. It is nothing.' The man's voice was fast disappearing into the darkness.

In India, people and animals live side by side, equal in their right to life. Everyone has to do the best they can.

The second day of the three-day fair was held at the polo ground. In the summer time the temperatures in Rajasthan can reach 50°C (120°F) – in the summer of 1999 over 200 people died as a result of record temperatures – but this morning was balmy at 25°C (77°F). Even so, tents had been erected to protect people from the sun and the wind whipping up the sand. The camels that were to play in the polo match came from the Border Security Force, the large, well-trained and no-nonsense military battalion. Rajasthan state borders onto Pakistan, and this means the combined problems of two countries, two major religions and an ancient and bloody, bitter rivalry. There is also the additional agitation of arms and drug smuggling, particularly heroin. The worst possibility is outright war. But today, the riders and their mounts were out for some fun. The camels were decorated with shells, bells, tassels on their chins and pearl necklaces known as ghorbands. They also had their fur clipped in beautifully executed swirling floral and geometric designs. The camels were so compelling that I wanted to touch them. I moved closer but was still a couple of metres away when they started to make small whistling noises. I stepped back respectfully.

The camel is a very important animal in India. It not only performs all sorts of domestic chores but also is the only creature that can withstand the immense temperatures of the desert. In the blistering heat of summer a camel can survive

Jaisalmer

without water for seven days but may lose up to 100 kilos or 25 per cent of its body weight. In the winter it can survive for nearly a month. The body temperature of a camel drops considerably during a cold night, allowing it to conserve energy.

Polo was the first contest and its seriousness was signified by the presence of the Prime Minister of India. (The Mogul emperor Akbar introduced the game of polo into India in the 16th century. It apparently originated in Persia.) One by one, the riders standing beside their camels were introduced. They wore very handsome outfits of white tunics and pants with a brilliant orange turban and cummerbund. Once the proceedings got under way, most of us didn't have a clue what was actually happening. Players tumbled to the ground, polo sticks went flying, camels fell on their callused knees but eventually someone won the game, indicated by a lot of shouting, smiling and shaking hands.

There were other contests – the most outstandingly decorated camel, and a seriously silly competition to see how many people could fit on top of a camel – but after three hours we decided to return to our hotel. We had now been in India for five days and Gaston was getting impatient to start painting.

At 4 p.m. he was ready to go. He has seen something of interest at the Gandi Chowk (town square or marketplace). After driving around for a bit and trying to park the car somewhere Gaston finally settled on putting his easel in a doorway, far enough back to get a good view of the subject: a gateway. He likes to paint archways and directly in front of him was an old entrance into the markets and shops. Dinesh radiated importance and pride as he carried the wooden paintbox and easel; finally, he understood what the box was, and was now all smiles. I guess what we should have done in the first place was to show it to him but we didn't think of it. It sounds ridiculous in retrospect.

I always stay somewhere near Gaston when he is working. He sometimes needs things, such as a cold drink or a plastic bag for his paint-stained paper. I discovered a craft fair with at least 30 stalls only a few metres from where he was working. To my great delight one stall had the beautiful bangles I had

A Brush with India

seen in Fatehpur. They were sets of eight wooden bracelets, all with different designs and they were very inexpensive. There were also tiny trinket boxes with sparkling 'gems' embedded in the lids. Another stall sold, for a small sum, puppets representing the desert lovers, Mumal and Mahendra.

The Kathputlis or Putli-wallahs are traditional puppeteers who make their living by travelling from village to village, giving shows. Sometimes they have to accept other work such as farm labouring or anything that might be available to make extra money. Nomadic, they travel in groups of up to 10 families, pitching their tents at night and walking the long necessary journeys. They supplement their income by making puppets to sell to craft fairs and tourists. The husband is normally the head puppeteer and the wife plays a musical instrument and sings. Most of their plays are love stories.

I would come back to the puppets and the bangles but wanted to see the woollen shawls at another booth. Ever since I had first seen shawls with pieces of mirror sewn into them, I had been intrigued. They were in all colours, each one nearly 3 metres long and they were a bargain. I especially liked a black shawl with tiny pieces of mirror sewn in with red thread, but the men at the stall were dismayed at my choice. Their women, so ravishing in bright colours, would never dream of choosing drab shades like black or navy blue.

Walking on, I noticed children's cheap toys, made of plastic. Bright green cars and trucks sat on makeshift tables. Interestingly, there was an absence of plastic swords, machine guns, rapid-fire artillery tanks or even water guns. I asked the price of a small green car and was surprised to find out it was nearly the price of a set of eight beautifully hand-made bracelets.

Unbearably hot, I decided to go back and see how Gaston was getting on. I found him exactly as I expected, totally surrounded by crowds of curious people. He had been concerned that he might not be able to paint in India. We have been in countries where people talked to him constantly, making it impossible for him to concentrate. Sometimes I've had to sit on the ground as close to him as possible, to ward people off. When he is painting, he is oblivious to what is going on around him, deep in concentration, and he resents intrusions. Once, when we were in Honfleur, France, a Japanese movie company asked if they could film him. His reply was that they could do what they liked as long as they didn't bother him. Surrounded by a team of 15 people, with lights and cameras rolling, he just went about his business as usual, totally unmoved or impressed by the idea he was going to be on Japanese television. Right now, he seemed fine: the local people, although intensely curious, were quiet and respectful.

Just around the corner were several small shops, one of which had refrigerated bottled water. I bought a bottle and went on to the next shop for some mentholated cough drops. When I went to pay, the shopkeeper asked me where I bought the water I was holding. It had a label I had not seen before but I thought it would be all right. It wasn't: I was told I should have kept to a well-known brand. 'It's up to you. Go ahead and try it, but I wouldn't.' He sold known brands of water and I could, if I wished, buy one from him. Was he only trying to get me to buy his water or did he, perhaps, have a point?

After giving the second bottle of water and cough drops to Gaston, I returned to the craft fair to buy some bangles and trinket boxes for Christmas presents, and also the black shawl. The price this time was higher but I reminded the seller that his partner had already offered it to me for less. We finally settled, and he laughed and happily wrapped my pretty shawl in a plastic bag. The two men insisted I sit and have a cup of chai with them. It was difficult to refuse. Sitting high up in their makeshift stall, the object of curiosity and giggles of every passing Jaisalmer woman, I sipped my tea. The shawl sellers were polite and kind but the heat was insidious. I thought of the English with their imported customs and their blasted penchant for hot tea even in these abysmal temperatures.

I bought the Mumal puppet. They say that you should barter in India but this is not an easy thing when you are not used to it. It feels uncomfortable: I didn't like to cheat anyone and I didn't want to be an easy touch either. Since the asking price was 100 rupees, I started at 50. The husband and his tiny little wife kept assuring me that it was 'very nice, very nice puppet'. We agreed on 70. As he wrapped the puppet in a blue bag, I asked if it was true that his wife had made the puppet.

'Oh, yes,' accompanied by a lot of head wobbling and smiles of assurance, 'very beautiful work, my wife makes very beautiful.' Yes, she did. I had to agree. I handed over the 70 rupees and started to walk off but returned after a few steps. 'Well, you are right, so I will give the other 30 rupees to this beautiful wife of yours.' Thinking about it later, I wondered if I caused trouble for that tiny wife. I hope not.

When we had been searching for a parking space earlier in the day we had driven up a narrow, dusty street where there was a bazaar, of sorts. The word bazaar means market and a market can consist of only two or three carts. This alley was obviously designed for the shopper with very little money. It probably looked the same hundreds of years ago. I knew Dinesh was looking after Gaston so now I headed back there. I was totally out of place.

I had taken a couple of long, straight skirts to India. The one I practically lived in was ankle length and had a discreet slit to the knee for easy movement. I am always concerned about not offending people by my clothes and I was aware that Indian women had skirts or saris to the ground and never had their arms bare to the shoulder. They did have their midriff exposed and sometimes lots of it – much more sexy than knobbly knees.

Walking along the old road and seeing what people were selling, I knew I was out of place and looked it. I hoped the skirt wasn't too revealing. My camera I kept in my hand, not dangling like a stethoscope on my chest. There were so many photos I wanted to take that I wished to be as invisible as possible.

There were all sorts of workers in the street bazaar. Dozens of men, sitting in long rows on small mats not much bigger then themselves, were shoe repairers. Their tools and equipment were placed neatly in front of them. Old pieces of car tyre were being cut to replace worn-out soles: it seemed quite efficient, but there were so many men doing the same thing, I wondered how they could all survive. On the other side of the narrow road were the blacksmiths wearing gold earrings and neatly dressed in impeccable, improbable white. They sat low on their haunches, their legs bent back in impossibly sharp angles so that their knees touched their faces. A constant sharp ring

Jaisalmer

of metal against metal sounded out in short staccato rhythms. The black soil, steel hammer and anvil, and the soot-covered ground made a striking contrast to the brilliant bright red from the fire. I pointed to the camera and nodded my head up and down and then from side to side to make sure. A beaming smile, and 'Yes'. The people were so kind and so helpful, as I was to find the Indians everywhere. Here especially, with the difference in our lives so vast, I appreciated and felt humbled by their good nature and acceptance.

Two little boys sitting in the dirt waved me over to look at their little toy, a plastic remnant of the toys I had seen in the market. Their mother was working in a makeshift plywood box, elevated some 60 centimetres off the ground. In an area no bigger than 1.5 by 2 metres (5 by 7 feet), she was surrounded by huge stacks of clothes. She was a professional ironer, working with a cinder-filled iron as there was no electricity. On the left was the father, who had a small stall with little odds and ends such as pins and shaving blades. One of the boys chatted away to me in Hindi, oblivious to my inability to understand one word. I sat on the ground and played with the little toy, admiring it and making a big fuss. We all laughed and smiled. Asking if I could take a picture broke the spell: the little fellows were not at all sure about the camera. It was time for me to leave and when I shook their hands, they understood and waved goodbye.

I knew exactly what to do: I rushed back to the craft fair and the toy stall. There was a train set I had not seen before with three carriages, a little track and a key. It was just what I was looking for. After putting it in its box, the toy seller wrapped it in newspaper and put it into a blue plastic bag. Then I bought a large bottle of cold orange drink and raced back to the family. The mother saw me coming and smiled. I handed her the orange drink and her husband came over to see why I had come back. I gave the train to the parents and pointed to the children. The father took it and sat on the ground with the boys. I would have loved to see their expressions but I couldn't watch. I couldn't stay. I turned my head and walked quickly away. Behind my back I heard a high-pitched noise, squeals of pleasure made by two little children, sitting in the dust in a back road in Jaisalmer. I know I will be able to recall that sound forever.

By the time I got back to Gaston he was just finishing his painting. There were 20 men crowded behind him, watching intently. He had produced an intense, colourful impression of local life and I was happy for him because often the first painting is the hardest. I heard a young man profusely thanking him for 'letting me watch as it was so very revealing and of interest to me'. Dinesh, our man of few words, had a grin from ear to ear and wouldn't let anyone near the paintbox.

Later that night we walked up to the Jaisalmer fort like two aged hippies ready to enjoy life, whatever happened. Cars are not allowed into the fort, so it was blissfully quiet, magical, unchanged. We entered through a narrow stone portal surrounded by an 18-metre (60-foot) stone wall. The fort was built eight centuries ago by a Rajput warrior, in exchange for loyalty and taxes and the local people came here for protection against Moslem invaders. We wandered off into narrow lanes, into a myriad of tiny streets, and climbed up into the old houses, four to five storeys high. Distant views of infinite desert stirred our imagination with images of caravans and camels, the Silk Road and the world's richest treasures. Stone carvings of birds and flowers, so intricate they looked as though they were made of wood, adorned the doors and windows. The setting sun turned the colour of the walls all shades of pink and soft yellow; a warm desert wind flowed through the delicate latticework of stone.

We found a restaurant with the unlikely name of 8 July. Famous, it has accommodated every hippie-wanderer who has passed its way. We walked up some rickety ancient wooden stairs and marvelled at the view of the Jain temple just opposite. We shared a table out on the deck with two youngsters with thick English accents who were bumming around India. Gaston's eyes were riveted on a huge pile of thick greasy fries and the bottle of ketchup: real food. We ordered by number from the incredibly stained and grubby menu. I should have taken it as a souvenir as it must have been an original. Yes, Gaston could have a beer, but it was against the law to serve alcohol so close to the nearby temple, so would he mind if it was served in a teapot?

High in the fort are seven exquisitely carved Jain temples, known for their ancient manuscripts, approximately 800 years old. The library contains over 2000 manuscripts but it is not open to the public. Everything within the temple is clean and serene in contrast to what you might see in a Hindu counterpart. For a token fee, the temples, which are connected by common walkways, can be visited only in the morning. As in most public sites the most expensive part about getting in is not your body but your camera and, worse, your video camera: you are charged for them. We were not put off by the fact that our entrance fee was many times more than the local residents were asked to pay.

At first the religions of India seem overwhelming, but taken like a fine whisky, small sips at a time, they have a depth that makes you want to know more.

The Jain temples in Jaisalmer were built some time between AD1300 and 1600. The religion started around 575 BC, with a young man by the name of Vardhamana who was born of wealthy parents in the region of Bihar; his father was the clan's leader. But the boy was not destined to have an easy time. His parents belonged to an exclusive religious sect that believed reincarnation was nonsense and suicide the best way to end life. When he was 31 years old, his mother and father killed themselves by starving to death. Vardhamana decided he needed to do some serious thinking about his life. He threw away all his possessions, including his clothes, and wandered around naked to seek clarification of life's mysteries. He thought and talked about it for 13 years and came up with a set of ideas that appealed to many people. Deciding his concepts were inspired his disciples made him a Jina, a rarely seen special teacher: jinas include such people as Jesus, Buddha, Michelangelo and Einstein. His followers also decided he needed a new image and came up with the name of Mahavira, or Great Hero. By the time he died in 527 BC, his sect numbered about 14,000.

Mahavira was just one of a host of prophets who were trying to change religious conditions at that time. Simultaneously in history a huge cast of religious giants was coming to the fore: Jeremiah in Israel, Confucius in China, Zarathustra in Persia and the great Siddhartha Gautama, the Buddha, in India.

What do Jains believe? One concept, which tourists in India are often forced to think about, is that something is true but only from a particular point of view. Other points of view are true from a different perspective. Another concept: there is no such thing as time, because time is eternal and formless. Indian people have a very different attitude to time, which can be exasperating for a person from a Western culture. Our driver, for instance, did not wear a watch, although he was always 'on time' for us. Many Indians don't wear watches by choice.

The dogma of Jainism teaches that the universe has existed for all eternity and any changes that have occurred are due to nature and not to human beings. Having disposed of God, Jains replaced him with high achievers of the sect: monks and religious hermits. These philosophers were accepted as mentors but not as divine. Jains believe that the only way to escape reincarnation is to lead a blameless life. To be a Jain means taking five vows: not to kill any living thing, not to lie, not to take what is not given, to preserve chastity and to renounce pleasure in all external things. Jainism, meaning a person who overcomes, practices the most extreme form of non-violence called ahimsa. Sensual pleasure is a sin, always. The philosophy is indifference, both to pleasure and to pain. A Jain must learn to become detached from all things. A Jain cannot become a farmer or agriculture worker because he might inadvertently kill some insect in the ground. A good Jain will not eat honey as it represents the lifework of a bee. He also strains water, in an attempt to filter out any living organism. You can often recognise a Jain in the street because he is wearing a mask to cover his mouth, so that living creatures are not inhaled and accidentally killed. A devout Jain will sweep the path in front of him and put shades on lamps in case crazed creatures fling themselves against the light. Jains are the strictest of vegetarians and can never slaughter an animal, for any reason. Jains set up special hospitals and rest homes, such as the one in Delhi, feeding and caring for elderly animals, until they die.

Their intense regard for life is a noble one but side by side with it is the astonishingly contradictory belief that the only life they can take is their own. Suicide is believed to be the greatest victory: the victory over the will to live. The preferred method is starvation.

Basic to Jainism is universal tolerance and a belief in total non-criticism. Gaining new members or spreading the faith is not important to a Jain. Today, in Rajasthan, about 40,000 people practise Jainism and there are about six million Jains in the world, most of them residing in India. This is a living religion with both practising monks and nuns living in the Jain temple in Jaisalmer. As always, visitors are requested, to leave their shoes outside the front door.

The following day was the third and last day of the Jaisalmer Desert Festival. Fireworks were planned for the evening, 42 kilometres away at the Sam Sand dunes, a popular excursion from Jaisalmer. It is at Sam Sands that camel safaris can be hired for one day to four days: as well as your own dromedary, meals and bedding are supplied. The quality of the food is in direct relationship to the amount paid for the tour. Apart from the sheer romance of riding a camel in the desert there are interesting things to see – goatherds and old ruins, animals like the Chinkara antelope and tiny desert birds – and the immense stillness of the desert to be experienced.

We heard from our new friends, the Prataps of Hyderabad, all the great things about Sam Sands, but we never made it. When we told them we were leaving, Vijaya took off one of her toe rings which I had found so attractive and insisted I wear it. It was her gift to me. She had also given me some bindis to wear on my forehead. Vijaya was one of the few women who made a point of talking with me. We were two women who could learn from each other. I wish I had realised it was I who needed to take the initiative. The men were always interested and helpful but women seldom spoke or even looked at us directly.

During the night Gaston developed a fever. I had no idea what it was. When we were so far from home and knew that the medical service was so primitive, an illness seemed frightening: it could have been a stomach upset or it could have been typhoid. All I knew was that he had a high temperature and a deep cough. We had to leave and go on to the next destination: to find a doctor and medical care we could feel confident about. I certainly was not going to risk taking him to the hospital at Jaisalmer. Also, it was the morning of the last day of the festival. Tomorrow 10,000 tourists, Indian and foreign, would be heading east to Jodhpur, a day's drive away to the southeast. It was the only city of any size in the vicinity that had accommodation. If we didn't leave immediately, we probably would not find a room. Dinesh was happy we were on our way. He didn't like Jaisalmer.

Chapter 4

Jodhpur

We had driven almost as far west as we could go in India. Years ago, on another painting trip, we had camped in the Tongariro National Park, in the middle of the North Island of New Zealand. Although a desert, it is not as big as the Thar Desert and the weather is much kinder. Staying in a tent for several days, illustrated the profound beauty in a place that at first sight seems austere. The desert is not just beige or light brown or mono-colour: it is a special palette of clear, luminous colour in all shades of the rainbow. What appears barren is actually teeming with life – you just have to stand still long enough to observe it.

As we drove east, the land slowly began to change. First there were a few straggly trees, then a few bushes and further on actual crops. How welcoming it was to see the amazing variations of green. We passed a village with a large pond where naked children were washing the broad backs of black buffalo. The water looked inviting. The heat was enough to bring out a slight sweat and I felt like swimming, even though the water was dark and soupy.

I love to read and follow maps; my sense of direction is excellent. My father taught me to pay attention to things on the road. 'Did you see that church on the last corner? What religion was it? Where was the last gas station? If it's 20 miles to Santa Rosa, how many more miles is it to Gurneyville? Do you remember where we buy the cherry cider?' He made such a great game of it. I'm old enough to say that I still remember the Burma Shave signs. If you don't know what I'm talking about, you missed a great American roadside ritual. The collective little rhymes, told in successive signs, made up a catchy story, which we each had to yell out as the car raced by. In India it seemed to me that each village was an exact copy of the one we had just seen. The road, which might have been in good shape for the last 50 kilometres, would suddenly deteriorate into dirt and dust. Cars, people and trucks would block the streets. Flashes of pale hands and flares of brilliant red from oxyacetylene torches were the only relief from black oil-covered men and earth. Once past the metal benders a sudden parade of colour and life followed with vendors of all descriptions selling fruit and vegetables, saris and children's clothing made from thin material in old-fashioned designs. Tiny matchbox cubicles of precious recycled wood offered matches, foil-wrapped aspirin and cough drops, which were hung like crepe paper at a birthday party. String beds supported men at rest. Large circles of other men, holding cards close to their chest hardly looked up as we passed by. Scattered throughout the crowd, women wore their iridescent gowns. Some wore a length of material called an odhni, a long veil pulled over their head to hide their faces. This custom of modesty picked up from the Moguls hundreds of years earlier, is not part of the Hindu culture but a Moslem concept. Semi-naked children played in the dirt along with feral dogs and hairy snorting pigs. Then gradually the scene would be reversed and we would be out on the bitumen again.

Sometimes we needed directions. If we asked a local he would go into long and very specific detail. If we asked a policeman he would frown and grunt, bend down just enough to see who was in the car, then flick a desultory finger in some direction. Our driver had to be desperate to ask a policeman. Maps were a great mystery to Dinesh and others we talked to along the road. Their excitement at being offered one to peruse was closely followed by a look of wonder and bewilderment.

Jodhpur is a city of nearly a million people. The approach from the north is a maze of alleys and impossibly narrow streets filled with incredible chaos. The main road coming from Jaisalmer, which took us over the pass and down into the city, was 10 kilometres (6 miles) of misery. It was only slightly wider than a goat track and had long ago lost its bitumen. It was now only dust, dirt and deep holes. When trucks, and buses approached our car, I had no idea how it was possible for them to get around us, other than squeeze us off the cliff side. To add to our apprehension, Gaston and I were convinced that Dinesh was lost. But suddenly Meherangarh Fort appeared, towering and massive on the hill overlooking Jodhpur. To see

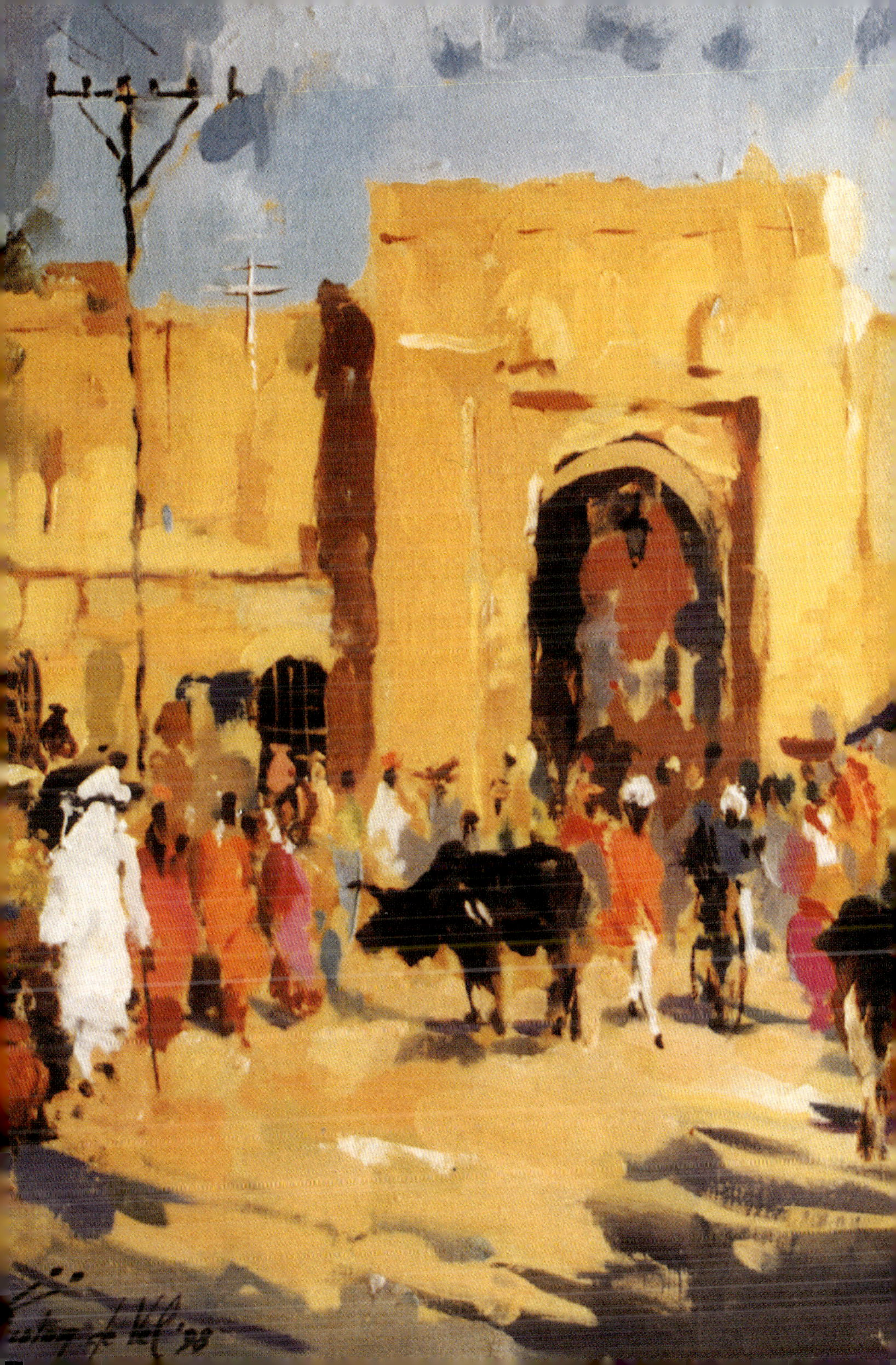

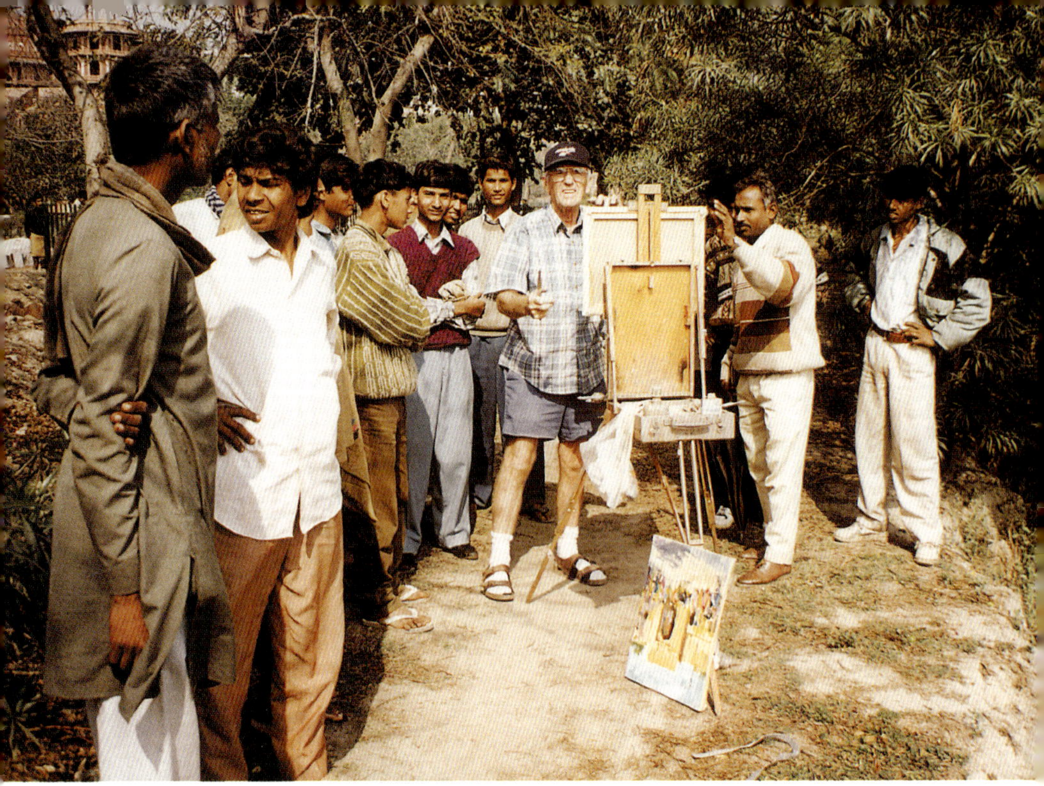

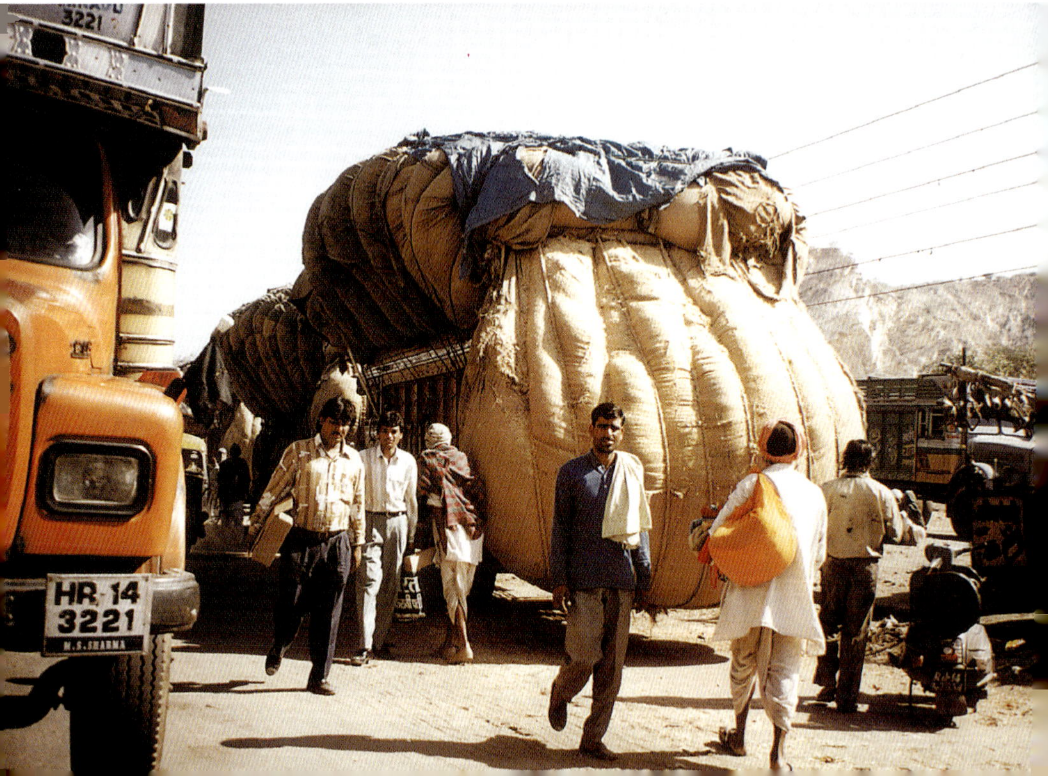
3221
HR 14
3221

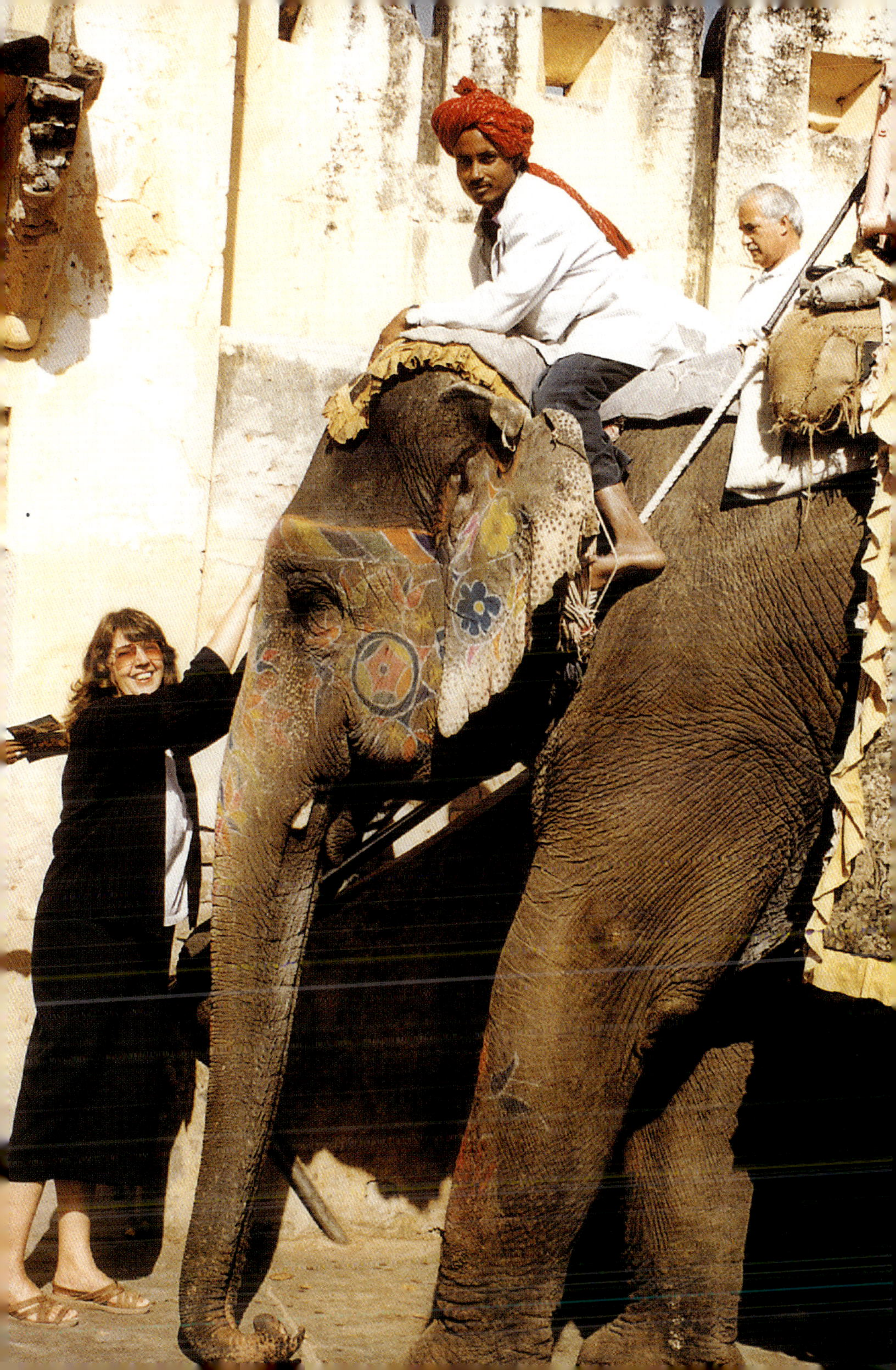

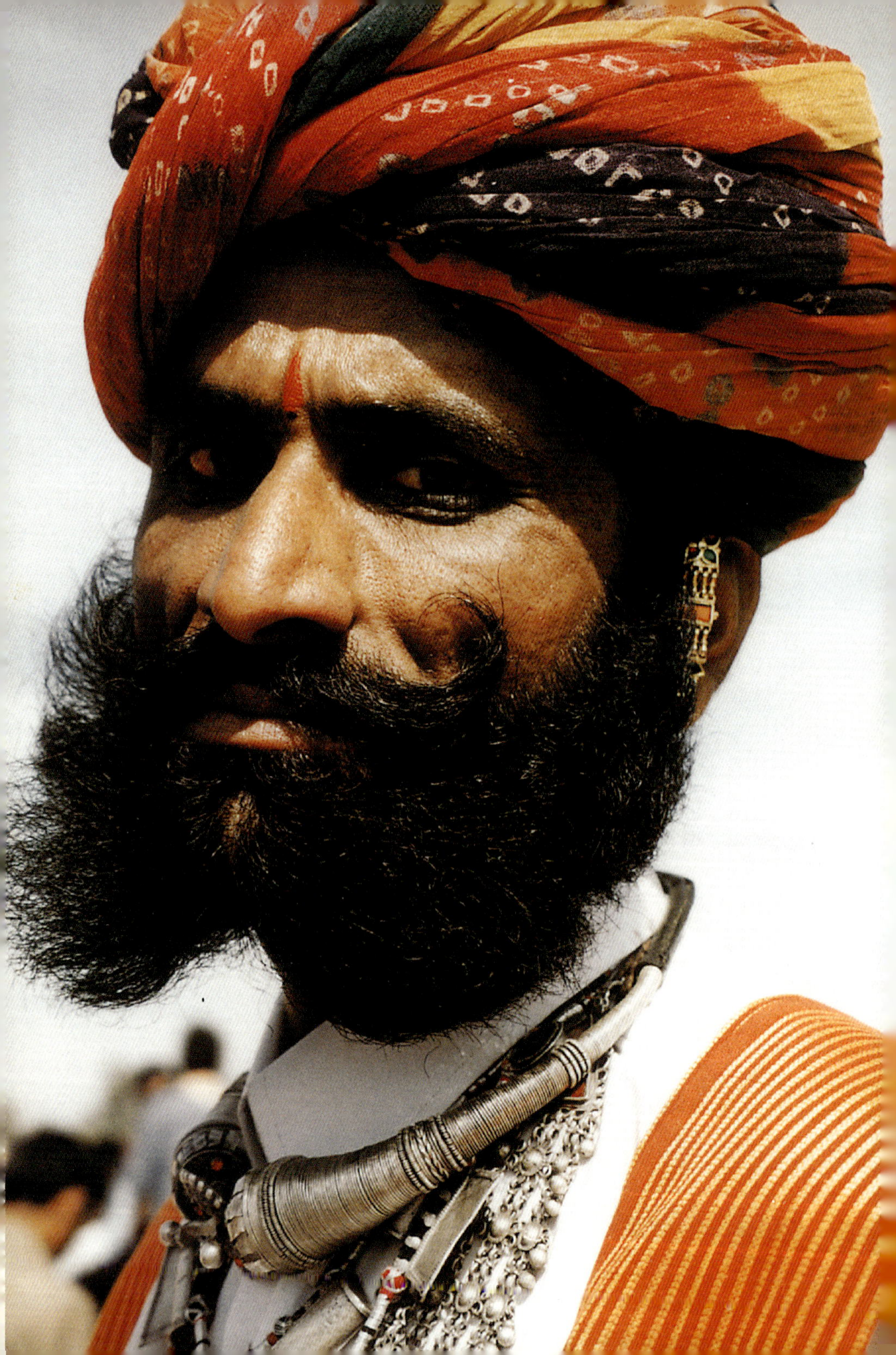

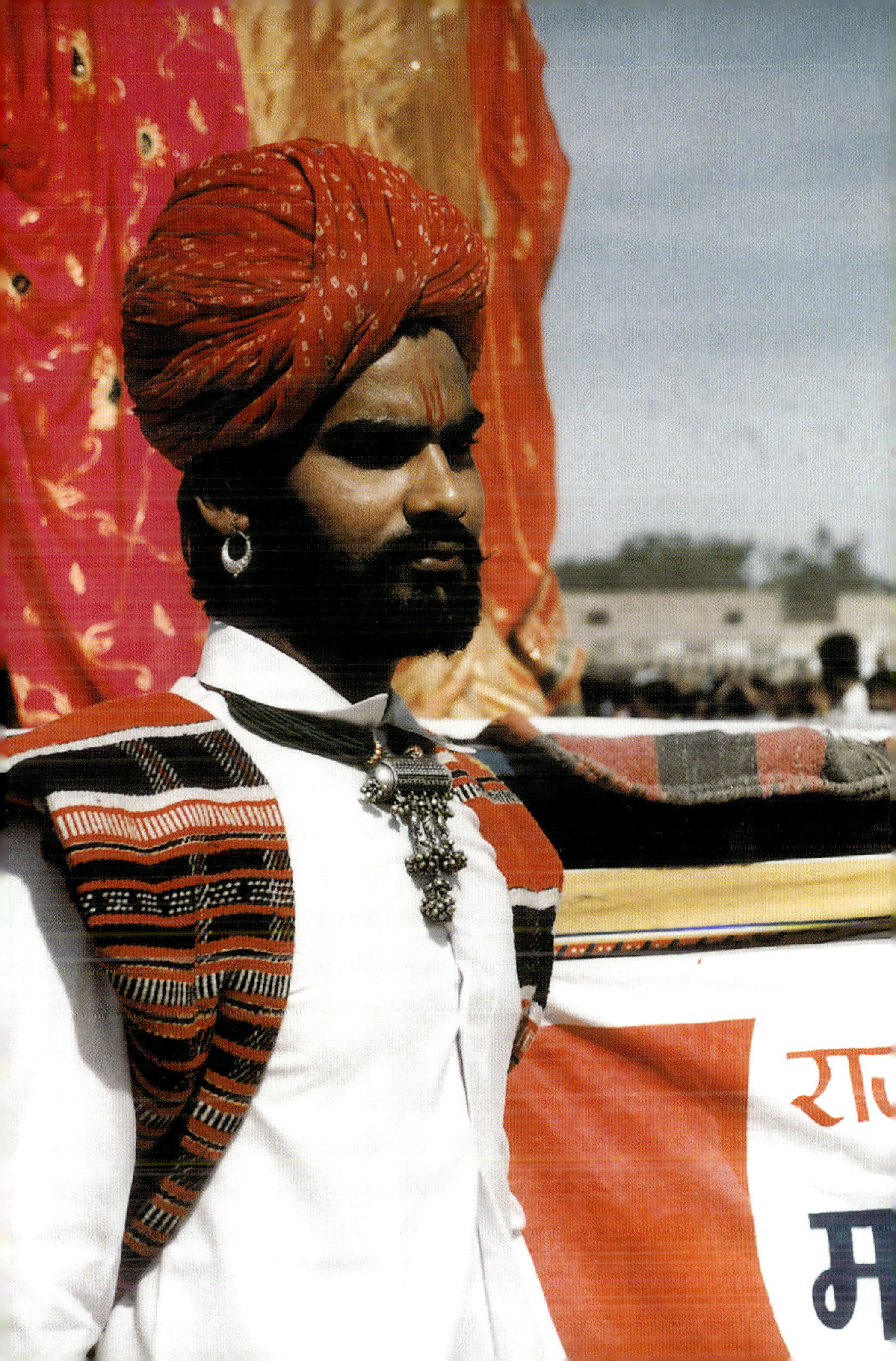

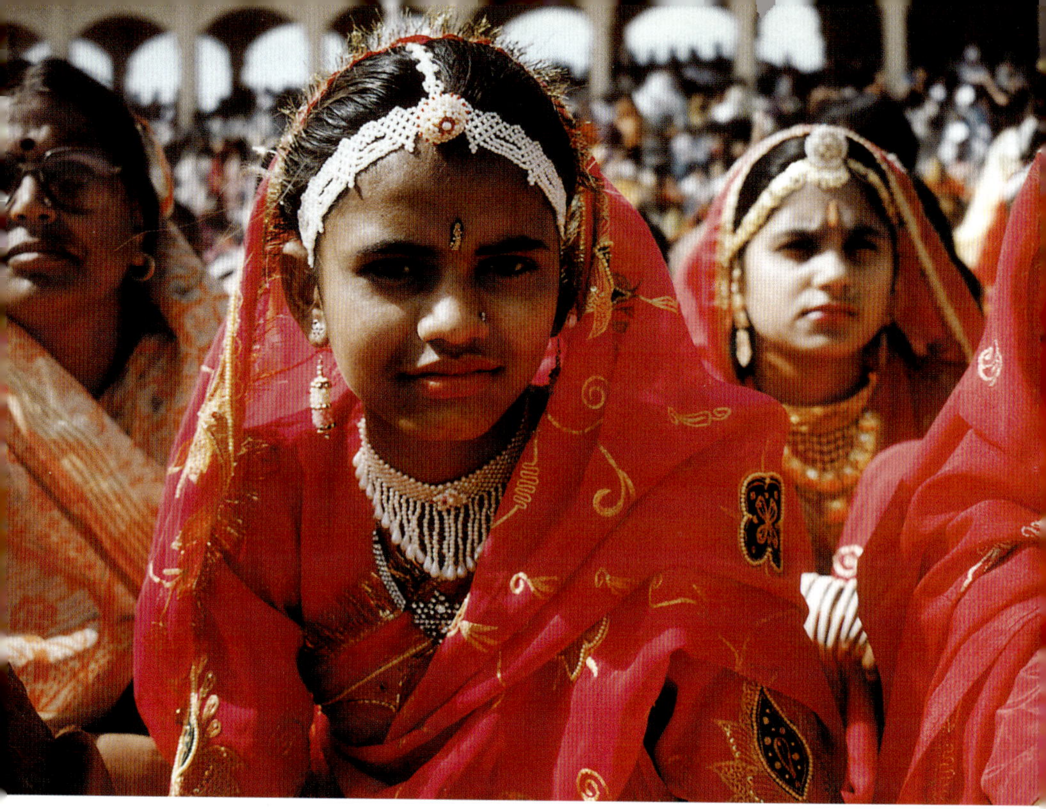

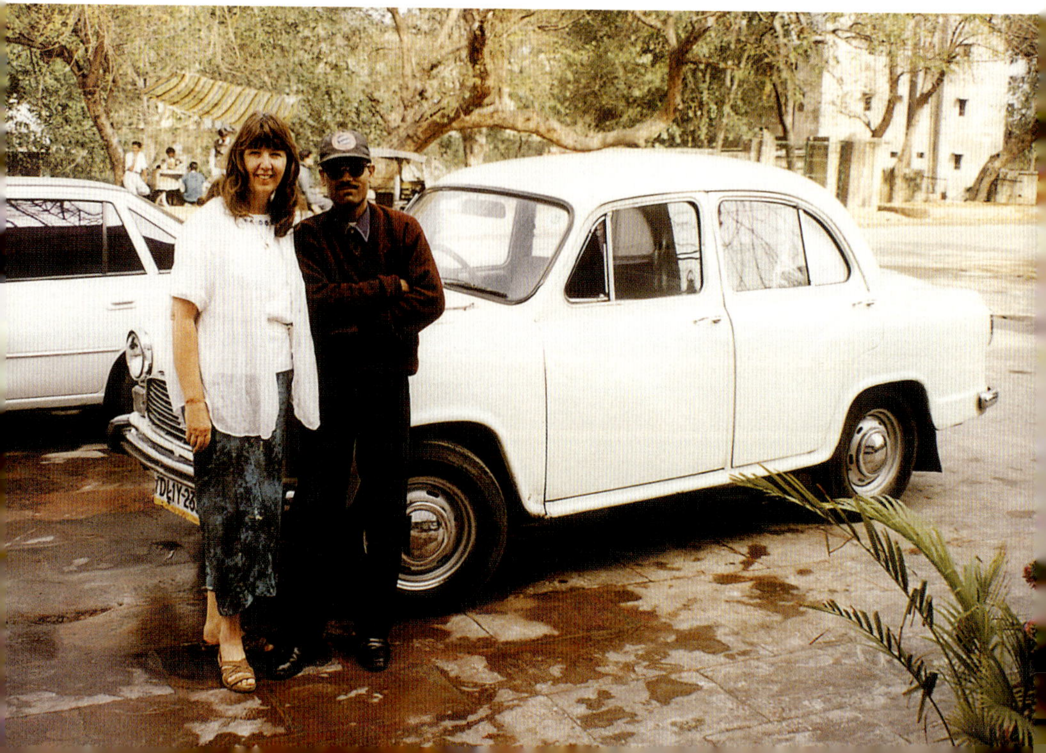

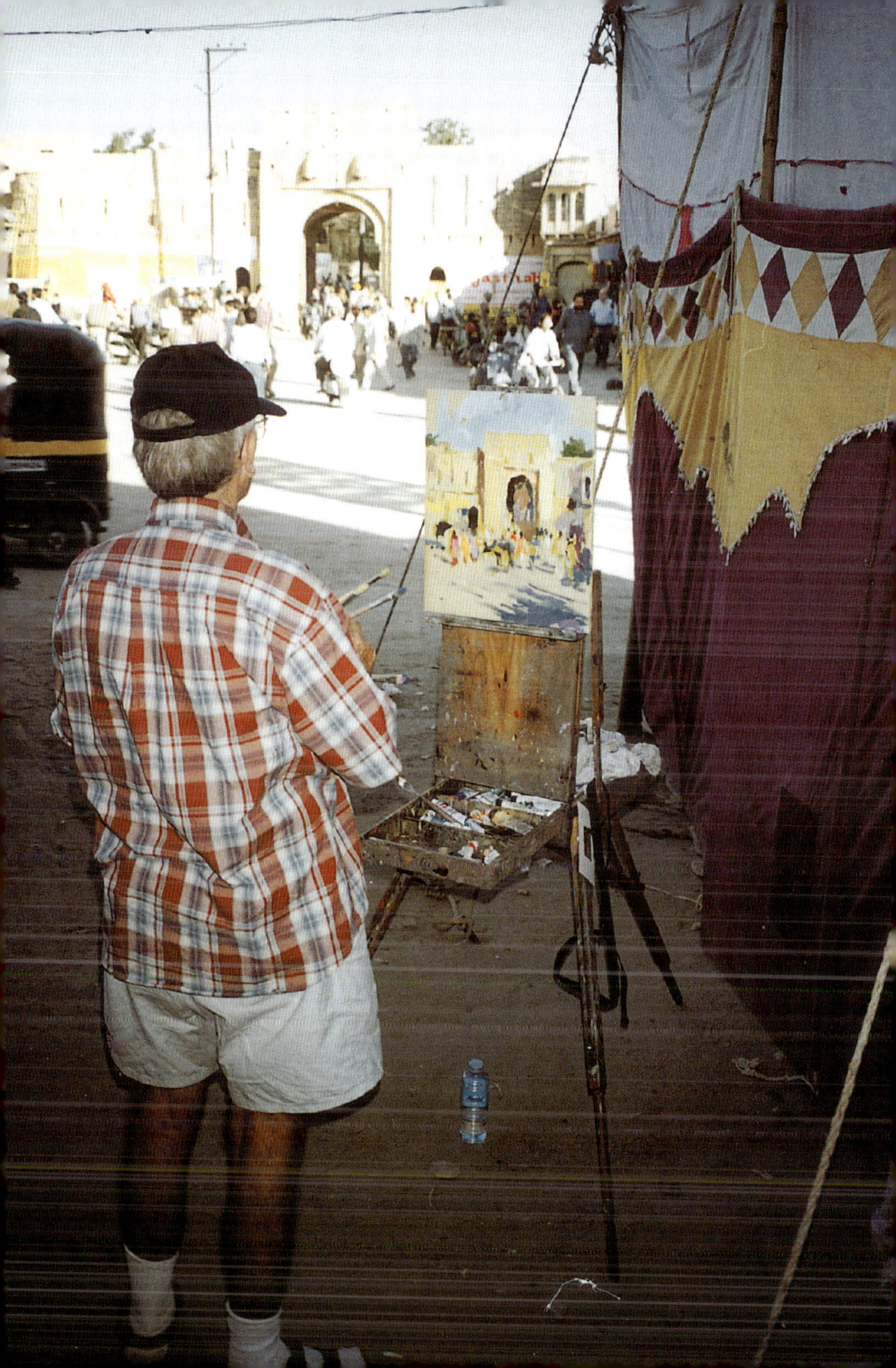

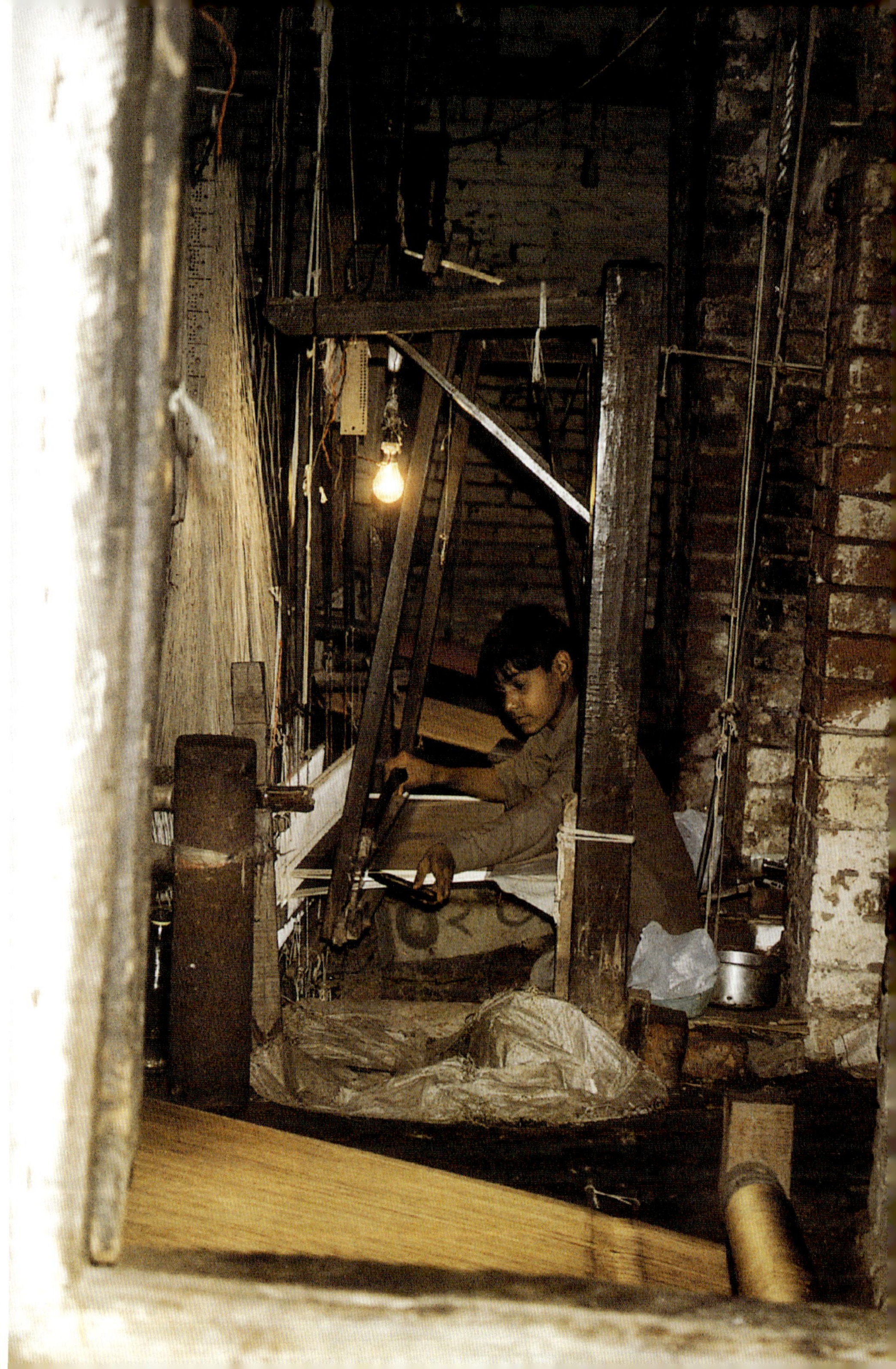

Jodhpur

it is to understand the strength of the chiefs of Rajasthan. It dominates everything, by both its size and its site.

It took us some time to find the hotel we had carefully picked out in our travel guide. Choosing hotels from a book is like buying a ticket in a lottery, with just as many chances that something good will come from it. Our book said it was a 'good choice' and 'near the Sojati Gate'. It sounded comfortable and, since it was on the 'outskirts of town', possibly quieter. Finding the place was a nightmare. One building in ten had a number on it and the numbers on one side of the street had nothing to do with those on the other. The bedlam of downtown Jodhpur was unimaginable. In every possible space the inevitable carts sold clothes, shoes, make-up, hair products, – anything, everything, you could think of. Endless numbers of vendors were selling food, fried balls of this and pastry squares of that. Candy and sweets were enormously popular. There were literally thousands of carts in front of thousands of shops with a street full of camels, donkeys, pigs foraging, dogs barking and great Brahma bulls lounging, prostrate, in the middle of the road. Added to this was the heat and congestion of cars, buses, mopeds, motorcycles and never-ending throngs of people. The noise caused an instant headache, the choking fumes blocked the sinuses and momentary tears welled up because the hotel we had hoped would be our refuge was fully booked. Gaston was now very sick and I was not sure what to do next.

Dinesh did. We left the centre of town and drove to the Ghoomar, which was a RTDC, Rajasthan Tourist Development Corporation, hotel. The rooms all looked the same but the prices were different depending on the floor you were on. The ground floor was the most expensive and had a room available. I took it. It was large and had a window, although barred, which looked into a dusty garden with a few trees. There did not seem to be any mosquitoes. We had a television set but as usual it didn't work. Our room service attendant was overjoyed with our arrival and immediately suggested tea. Gaston went to bed shaking with fever but was comforted by the clean, cool sheets and good mattress. The tea was brought by our beaming porter whose hand automatically flipped palm up every time he let go of a tray.

A Brush with India

What Gaston wanted most was a cool drink but the hotel could only supply tepid lemonade. I had noticed, in front of the hotel, a small stall selling ice cream and cold drinks. The proprietor must have known a thing or two because yes, he did sell cold lemonade but it was three times the price of warm lemonade. I bought four drinks and an ice cream and the smiling vendor packed up for the night and went home.

The next morning Gaston was too ill to get out of bed. He refused a doctor, preferring to wait another day. I had asked our driver to be at the hotel at nine and decided I might as well have a look at Meherangarh Fort. At least I could see if there was a possibility for painting, if and when Gaston was feeling better.

The return trip up to the fort was 5 kilometres (3 miles). Asking Dinesh to come back at 12.30, I walked up to the first of the heavy iron gates. Of enormous height, they were heavily studded with iron spikes to dissuade elephants, used as battering rams, from crashing their way into the fort. The walls were over 20 metres (68 feet) wide and in some places nearly 36 metres (117 feet) high. The entrance for foreign tourists was on the right, for locals on the left.

It was a long steep walk between the walls and the seven successive gates to Iron Gate, the final entrance. It would not have been physically possible for a herd of elephants or a horde of men to run all the way to the top and bang the last gate down. By the time they got to the top their lungs would have imploded. The morning was wonderfully clear and provided an outstanding opportunity to take photographs of the blue city of Jodhpur. In the beginning only Brahman, the highest caste, were allowed to paint their houses blue. When there was a war, because of their high status as priests, their lives and houses were spared. Today the houses are painted blue because it is pretty and distinctive. In the summer when the average temperature is 40° C (102°F) it looks cooler and it is also believed to discourage mosquitoes. Whatever the reason, the houses looked like blue silk against the deep brown of the surrounding desert.

Touts appeared along the way asking if I would like to visit their shop. Did I need film? 'Best price, very best price, for you.' What about water, postcards, antiques? An old man

Jodhpur

and a small boy began to play a fragile stringed instrument, a primitive form of the sarangi, which makes high-pitched but not unattractive music. I stopped to listen. They stopped playing. Now that they had my attention, they wanted to sell me the sarangi. It was an unsuccessful exercise for both of us. As I climbed further up the smooth, sand-coloured road, another played the flute and a tiny young girl, dressed in red and gold, danced for my pleasure and my rupees. She swayed her hips. Her diminutive arms caressed the air. She was direct in her gaze and erotic in her manner. I know I made a judgement without knowing the circumstances, but I could not give her, or more exactly her father, money. I felt angry, too influenced by my own culture to get past the idea that sexual innuendo in an eight-year-old is appropriate.

'What if she's starving? Well, she doesn't look like she's starving,' I said to myself. 'Well, what if her father beats her if she does not bring in the expected rupees? I don't know.' I kept walking.

Before the last gate another group of men were playing the drums and the sitar. They, too, stopped and started depending on whether tourists passed by. Their music was sensual, strange and had the rhythm and cadence of the East. It was a sound that involuntarily produces the desire to close one's eyes and sway to the music. The drumbeats were primitive, ancient, an irresistible code. I imagined myself sitting on an elephant in a velvet-covered, jewel-encrusted howdah, about to enter into the palace.

Reality returned when I paused to look at the handprints on the wall, just after the entrance gate. When Maharaja Man Singh died in 1843, his body was carried through this portal. As he passed under it, his 15 wives placed their oil-stained hands on the sandstone wall. This was their last action. One by one, in accordance with the honour of the Rajputs, they threw themselves into their husband's funeral pyre. Not long after, a sculptor carefully hollowed out the handprints. The tiny, delicate hands, now forever embedded in the wall, are another stark and frightening reminder of sati. For a long time this was a place of adoration, but worship is now forbidden. Sati can have no redeemable qualities for women today, but for Rajput women of another time, it was a way to show their own honour

A Brush with India

and their courage. Looking at the hand prints brushed in blood-red powder, I tried to imagine the courage it would take to lay my head in the arms of my dead, burning husband.

The best museum I saw in Rajasthan was here in Meherangarh Fort. Not only was it well presented, but I had my own personal guide. My entry ticket said, 'Please do not tip our staff. If you wish to show your appreciation, a contribution to the Staff Welfare Fund can be placed in the gratuity box at the booking office.' It seemed ironic that, of all the people I had met, these guides, more than most, deserved a tip for their politeness. We walked up and down four floors and sometimes through rooms two or three times. My guide was limping from a recent accident, but still he was friendly and eager to answer my questions.

Some places have a presence that envelops you like an invisible coat. The spirit of Meherangarh was warm and sociable: there must have been much love and laughter here. How could I believe this, when very young women were incarcerated behind these walls for their entire lives? I felt it with certainty. My Armenian grandmother was married at 13. Although she later became an emigrant to the United States, she longed for her former home and the ways of her people. She died before I was born but left behind a small book about her life: without it I would never have known her. I went to visit her birthplace and I wept. I wept because I understood why her photos always seemed sad: she just wanted to go home.

There were clues about life as it was here. Seeing the royal baby cradles was to know how much these little infants were loved. In these cribs, completely fashioned in gold, velvet lined and covered in paintings of flowers, the babies could be rocked all day long. It is said that Indian people have such wonderful dispositions not because of their religion but because they are the most adored children on earth.

Just across from the Zhanki Mahal, where the cradles were, was a special room, the Pearl Palace, which was used as a conference hall. Here the maharaja met with his warriors, tribesmen and his statesmen of Rajasthan. The ceiling was made of fragrant sandalwood and enhanced by glass tiles and gold filigree. All around the room were small alcoves that

Jodhpur

originally held oil lamps. The reflections from the golden ceiling, the flickering soft light and the coolness of the white marble floors and walls must have led to long convivial conversations. The maharaja who had the room constructed included, behind the long back wall, a secret passage accessible only from the zenana or women's apartments. Here the maharaja's wives could sit and listen to the men's conversation without being seen.

The Phool Mahal or flower room was where the maharaja was privately entertained. Groups of professional dancers came here to dance for the king's pleasure. He hired a famous artist to make the room a visual perfection. Enormous, flared, golden columns supported a ceiling embellished with 8 kilograms (17 pounds) of gold plate. Every centimetre of the room was covered in paintings of flowers and birds and delicate designs. When the artist died unexpectedly, rather than employ someone else to finish the job, it was left unfinished in respect for the artist.

The zenana, were revealing in their design. The maharaja, who reigned from 1843 to 1873 had 35 wives. He had a huge bed placed in the centre of his bedroom so the view of the city far below could be fully enjoyed. Above the bed was an enormous, embroidered velvet fan. On an outside wall was a rope attached to the fan. To cool the room a servant only had to pull the rope up and down and a gentle breeze filled the room, providing instant air conditioning with no buzz of electricity. Wives had to be very nice to the eunuchs, who were in their care: perhaps even a gift or two might be given for certain favours. The chief eunuch was the one to say whether a certain lady might be indisposed or not. Since eunuchs came, as children, from the poorest of families, they had little to lose and a great deal to earn. Some became inordinately wealthy but, owing to delicate, if not perilous, working conditions, were severely inclined to the liquid friendship of early Rajasthani Johnny Walker. Blue label, of course.

When I left the museum, I didn't give my guide a tip and for the rest of the day I regretted it. He was worth it: he even went out of his way to take me up a steep ladder to show me a mother vulture feeding her two little chicks, on the outside wall of the Fort.

A Brush with India

Once outside the museum, I continued to the top of the fort where the cannon and ramparts are located. Along the way, tiny squirrels ran excitedly over the path and up the exquisitely carved sandstone walls of the palaces. Because of its colour, the sandstone looked remarkably like old and weathered wood. There was a garden near the top and a horse tethered under a tree. Right at the top was an outstanding view of Jodhpur. In the distance, Umaid Palace rose up out of the land, casting silhouettes of minarets and round domes, piercing the smudged blue and pink skyline. I walked to the edge of the wall and looked down. I could see the city, strikingly beautiful and massive. More incredible was the sound of a million people carried by air currents: huge, overwhelming and like nothing I had heard before. It was every voice and yet it was only one. It was a vision of the past, of history. It was a revelation of the future. Shortly after the year 2000, India was expected to surpass the population of China.

Dinesh was late, but then perhaps I was early. Neither of us wore a watch. In the busy parking lot was a young boy whose every need in life would be met if I would let him shine my shoes. Since I was wearing sandals, I wondered what he could possibly do with them and I brushed him away with a wave of my hand. I walked around the parking lot and looked over the edge of the mountain pass. Biding my time, I continued to watch the shoeshine boy and tried to find out his success rate. Not one person let him shine their shoes. Not one soul kindly slipped him a few rupees. He was just a dark-skinned boy dressed in rags with no shoes of his own. He came back to me. I sat on my haunches with him and we talked. He asked me for a peen (pen). I could see our car coming through the gate. Dinesh did not approve of my giving money to beggars so I turned away and carefully took out 20 rupees. Surreptitiously, hand behind my back, I handed it to young mister shoeshine. We shook hands and said goodbye. I thought I would never see him again.

On the way home I bought some bananas and a papaya from the bazaar. I had no way of knowing whether I was paying the right price but inevitably someone always came along to haggle for me. Occasionally, there would be quite

Jodhpur

an argument but it was always resolved with the 'best price', my unknown benefactor apparently getting his satisfaction from the fact that justice had been done. Or perhaps, as some cynics have pointed out to me, the benefactor and the seller split the difference. Anyway, it was still cheaper then I would have paid in the first instance and it was quite good entertainment.

Back at the hotel Gaston managed to eat a little fruit but his temperature was still high. Starting to feel very apprehensive, I decided that tomorrow, protest or not, we were going to find a doctor. We were such a long way from Delhi and the flight home. After lunch, Gaston just wanted to sleep, so the best thing for me to do was to go for a walk. Behind our hotel was a park and a zoo.

A woman doing anything by herself in Rajasthan is an oddity and needs to be investigated. The moment my dusty sandal stuck itself outside the gate of the hotel, every taxi, every auto-rickshaw, every tuk-tuk, in the street came to a screaming halt. This was a busy street, a main road into the city centre. I soon learned that smiling and waving a polite no thanks was completely useless. It only gave them the chance to make a pitch. They would come up with some implausible offer such as, for 5 rupees they would take you to 'many different places, you like, three hours, four hours no problem'. Along the way, they would just happen to make stops at their cousin's place, which just happened to sell saris, or jewellery. And if you were not tempted to buy something, over the next three hours their life history would be unfolded in such a way that by comparison you would feel like a rich, privileged capitalist. The 5 rupees would become 50 or 100 or 200, depending on how decadent and selfishly rich you were made to feel. The worst thing was their stories were almost certainly true and it was impossible not to feel compassion and sympathy opening up your wallet.

The way to avoid all this was to at least look as if you knew exactly where you were going, looking down at the ground and refusing to glance around. Unless you kept going resolutely ahead you would be vulnerable.

The zoo was directly behind our hotel: I could have gone left or right as it was one block either way to the entrance. It

A Brush with India

was a relief to finally find it because the noise from the horns on the tuk-tuks trying to get my attention was unnerving. Three boys about 10 years old were following me and had started to become a nuisance. They wanted money – an unusual experience and the only time it happened. They walked directly in front of me so that I sometimes had to push them out of the way. One little ratbag pinched me but the three of them ran away when I became angry. With relief I saw the entrance to the zoo and entered through the wire gate. The entrance fee was minimal but there was a registry book to fill out with the date, number of my ticket, my name, where I came from, how many people were with me and, as a final embellishment, my signature. I then received a white piece of paper with eight little squares. I had no idea what it all meant as no one spoke English.

I was directed into a large aviary. The birds were pretty but I found more pleasure in being away from tuk-tuks and the naughty boys than in the birds themselves. I did think the white peacocks had a certain amount of chic, though. After resting for a while, I found there were only birds in the cage and nothing else. Because the zoo was a series of cages separated from each other it was necessary to walk around the park and enter each cage through a set of double wire fences. I walked over to the next cage. It was half the size of a football field and contained one bear. Black, very old and lying on his back on the ground, he might have been handsome once, but you could see he was beaten, done, finished. All the hair on his back had rubbed off. He occasionally moved his head or waved a paw to let us know he was still alive.

I was so lost in my dark thoughts about caged animals that I jumped when a young man started to talk to me. 'Bear, yes, old yes, very old,' he beamed at me as if this pathetic animal was a national treasure. I knew he was showing off to his friends. He spoke English and they didn't. Or perhaps he was the one with the courage to speak English, while the others didn't. I shook his hand. We all did a lot of smiling. I tried my best to make it seem like he was the perfect scholar. We were now friends; all us were now friends. I even tried to convey that this was a great bear and, above all, a great zoo. At that moment I was also a great liar.

Jodhpur

I returned to the park path and just when I thought I was by myself, I was surrounded by a large group of school children. To my relief they were pure delight. They wanted to shake my hand, talk to me. Their smiles were radiant, warm, interested and interesting. Most people in India are so open and eager to know you. It is one of their greatest abilities: to make a person feel special. I wanted to know about their lives, be accepted by them and hear their stories.

The reason for the ticket with the eight little squares was my ticket got stamped every time I entered a cage. I wondered if this meant I could only go into a cage once? In case it did, I knew I didn't have anything to worry about.

The next cage, which held the big cats, was divided into two large pits. Behind these, in the centre, were a pair of impossibly small holding cages: one held a lion, the other a lioness. As the cages were in the middle, and hidden behind the little hills that led down into the pits, it was impossible for the gatekeeper to see them. There was no sign of any water for the cats and certainly no shade. I was thinking about leaving when I saw two boys, presumably members of the ratbag tribe, throwing stones at the lion. I yelled at them to stop it, right now and, to my surprise, they did – until I was out of sight and then they began their torture all again. The lion let out an enormous bellow and lunged at them. As the cage was only about 2.5 square metres in area, the king of the jungle smashed his head against the bars and fell back on his haunches. Just what the boys were watching out for. At least the lion still had spirit. By the looks of her the lioness had gone mad. She was lying very still in an adjoining cage. I talked to her in a gentle quiet voice. I took off my sunglasses and sat on the ground so my face was level with hers. I quietly repeated her eye movements: I blinked when she did or did she blink when I did? Her eyes started to enlarge and finally notice me. I had her attention. She didn't move. Neither did I. We stared at one another and then slowly her eyes lost focus. She turned away, knowing I wasn't important and I couldn't do anything about her life. I ran all the way out.

As I rested on a white marble bench, I could not believe it when the same three boys made a beeline for me, again. The public library was a few steps away so I walked quickly towards

A Brush with India

the door. Once I was inside, several dozen pairs of eyes met mine as they peered over the top of their newspapers. Clearly, I had again blundered into another awkward situation. I tried to bluff it out but the scene was so bizarre that I wouldn't have been at all surprised if the newspaper readers suddenly got on top of their gargantuan library tables and starting singing a song from the *Rocky Horror Picture Show*. The librarian was seated high on a platform at the end of a long table, like a high court judge, complete with gold-rimmed spectacles perched on the end of his nose. He scowled, obviously disapproving of my presence. The library books were in locked glass-fronted shelves. I kept walking. They kept staring. I had intruded into the private club of the men's newspaper readers library. Trying to appear nonchalant, I meandered down the aisles to look at the two side rooms. All the while, I was thinking, I have to stay here long enough for those boys to get tired and leave. But then, with one 'phoren' in the park, why should they leave? Head high but tiptoeing, I peeked into the other rooms, which again had more men sitting at long tables, reading newspapers. Along the walls and stacked up to the ceiling were thousands of yellowing, leather-backed books. They looked too old to be of much use other than for antique book dealers or sources of fuel. A quick glance showed that they were sets of law books, probably left over from the time of the British Raj. The newspaper-peepers were getting agitated so, unable to think of any further excuse for staying, I reluctantly left.

The boys had waited and I dreaded their constant chanting and bullying. I had another idea when I saw a group of well-dressed men standing in front of the small museum. I walked over as if I was going in. The brats knew the men would tell them off and they finally left. Luckily, I didn't see them again. To thoroughly confuse my feelings, as I left the park about 20 small, nicely dressed children, who had been playing together, came up to me. They wanted no more than to shake my hand and to say hello. They were so sweet and polite I wanted to hug them all.

Friday the 13th – how appropriate. Gaston was worse. His temperature was too high and I cursed myself for not ignoring his protests and getting to a doctor earlier. The management, although sympathetic, could only suggest that I take him to the hospital. I was not sure that was a good idea: it might expose him to more problems. Our guidebook suggested I should get in touch with an embassy or a five-star hotel to find medical advice. Right next to the Ghoomar Hotel was the official Jodhpur Tourist Bureau. When I had been in earlier to ask for a map the man was so abrupt that I hadn't thought about returning, but now I was desperate. Thankfully, someone else was in attendance this time and he immediately rang the doctor used by the Umaid Palace, a five-star-plus hotel. Dinesh and I gently bundled Gaston into the car, and with the personal guidance of the man from the tourist bureau, we arrived at the office of Dr Bhandari.

The rooms were small and narrow and there was a constant stream of patients. I was grateful that we were treated with special care and urgency. Ushering us into his office he told us he was the doctor for Umaid Palace and had treated many famous people who were always sending him 'presents in gratitude'. He also said he was a Jain and practiced Ayurvedic medicine – Auirveda means longevity – which specialises in natural cures. Ayurvedic doctors generally use a mixture of oils, herbs, crushed gems, extracts of flowers, fruit, gold and silver ash and other perplexing potions. 'Are we in trouble here?' I wondered. The sofa we sat on was so close that our knees touched his desk. He suggested we begin by both having a blood test, as I had a sinus problem. Now I was thinking, 'Blood test? Needles? India?' He looked deeply in my eyes and just at the point of embarrassment said, 'You don't have a sinus problem, you have a problem with your liver.' I tried to stay calm for Gaston's sake. After all, he was the sick one and if the doctor could at least tell me he was not seriously ill and prescribe something appropriate for him, all would be well.

We had our blood tests. The needles came in sealed packages – good start. Gaston went for an x-ray of his lungs in a room next door. We waited for a long time and the inevitable happened: I had to go to the toilet. I asked. Yes, it was the door on our right. Sordid, is the politest word I can think of to describe it. It was the hateful hole in the ground type and had never been cleaned from the day it was built: patches of brown made ominous patterns on the walls, hand basin and floor. Rising from a crouching position, I resolutely refused to let my clothes or hands touch anything. The price for these acrobatics was agonising leg spasms, but the pain was worth it. The taps had one inch of oozing grey grime around their base. There was no soap and no handtowels.

The x-ray came back. Gaston's heart was enlarged, but, 'Don't worry about it, it is just because you have been coughing so much. To be on the safe side I would recommend a test for your heart just to make sure it is nothing else.' This was a good idea and Gaston didn't have to go far – just to the second room down the hall. As I waited with the doctor in his office we chatted and he continued to tell me about all the miraculous cures he had made. I kept thinking of the toilet. While we waited, various patients came into the office. A pale young girl, holding a handkerchief over her mouth, sat next to me and started to explain why she was there. He frowned and, after examining her, gave her an injection. She returned and sat next to me again. He wrote out a lengthy prescription. Aimed at me, unavoidable because there was so little room, her sneezing and coughing made me feel like it was hunting season and I was the big goose.

When Gaston came back from having his ECG, Dr Bhandari explained to us that Gaston had viral bronchitis. He said it was common to visitors to Rajasthan because of the dust and the sand. He wrote out a prescription for antibiotics and said we should come back in three days if he was not better. We were also instructed to eat an apple plus a glass of milk every morning for the rest of our life. And every night for the next four to six weeks, I should boil 20 raisins and two figs with one cup of milk and one cup of water, until it was reduced by half. This would remove the impurities from Gaston's lungs.

When I got home to New Zealand, I half jokingly told my doctor about my liver problem and he suggested I have a blood test to dispel any doubts. It turned out I did have minor liver dysfunction. We now have the apple and milk every morning.

Knowing what the problem was lifted our spirits, and I even managed to get Gaston to eat a little, but I knew what was really bothering him: this was now day eight and he had so far managed only one painting. We only had three weeks

Jodhpur

more. For the first time in his life, this painting trip looked as though it was going to be a total failure.

So that I disturbed Gaston as little as possible while he slept, it was better for me to go out. But, as a lone woman in India, I had to find the courage to face the crowds again. This time I had the better idea of walking with the flow of the traffic rather than against it. The tuk-tuks, unable to see me properly, were not so merciless in their hopes for a fare. The dust rose in murderous clouds at each footstep. As always, it was a sunny, warm day. There were wonderful smells of incense and open fires where men were cooking chapatis and interesting-looking morsels for lunch. Fortune-tellers, with their sticks and implements spread out on blankets, sat earnestly talking to worried clients. The street was full of people and vehicles, animals and carts. Several blocks further I walked into what were obviously the law courts: there were several men in wigs and black coats. All along one side of the street were small open cubicles with a man seated in front of an ancient typewriter. If someone wanted to collect antique typewriters, this would be the place to come: old Olivettis and Coronas still hammered their fragile, metal keys onto paper. It was so hot and there was no place to sit, no shade. And as usual, there were only men milling about, frowning and wondering why I was there. Fed up, I went back to the zoo park, determined this time to sit somewhere, read my book and not look up. I would miss the nice people who only wanted to shake my hand and say hello but I needed to be peaceful and quiet. As I walked along I noticed, under the trees, men sleeping in the grass, wrapped in old blankets, managing somehow to cover both their head and their feet. Groups of men played cards, some were chatting to one another. I found a cool, white marble bench and settled down on one end to read my book about Rajasthan. It was obvious that men were staring at me, wondering what I was doing by myself in this park, but I didn't look up. I didn't answer questions. Inevitably, after five minutes, someone sat down next to me and stared patiently at my book.

'No way, I am not going to look at you. And I don't intend to answer your questions either,' I said to myself. He stayed. I kept reading. We were, I assumed, reading in tandem.

A Brush with India

He mumbled, 'Book? Ah! Rajasthan.' I would not be led into a conversation. No, definitely not. A second man sat on the arm of the bench, his body touching mine as he leaned down to read my book. When he started turning the pages I knew my solitude was just an illusion.

Okay, I thought, but I hope you're prepared for this woman 'phoren' because I have many questions.

No sooner had I surrendered than the three of us became 20. The belching in my ear I hardly flinched at. The closeness of so many men cheerfully smiling at me with blood-red, stained teeth from chewing betel nut, I looked right past. The crotches, which were constantly being reassured by their owner's left hand, a frequent Indian habit, I ignored. Right then, my bench seemed the most interesting place in the world to be.

Among all these men there were only two or three who spoke English. My answers to their questions were translated. I had just as many questions for them as they had for me. We were on the eve of an important election in India. What were their hopes? What did they want for their country? What were their most important political issues?

They answered by saying they wanted a man by the name of Atal Behari Vajpayee. He was born on Christmas day 1926. He was a founding member of the Bharatiya Janata Party, more commonly known at the BJP. I loved their enthusiasm, their excitement, generated by the discussion. This was a group of men who loved their country and had great expectations for the future, not only for Jodhpur or Rajasthan but for all India. They talked all at once but yet in accord. They informed me that Atal Bihari was 73 years old and had never been married. They seemed to think this was important, as if he had escaped a battle and should receive a medal of honour for getting to this age without being caught. He was described as an honest man. 'Honest, honest, honest,' repeated the entire group, down the line. 'Not a big cheater', I dutifully thought. Corruption, always the first word in a discussion on India politics, could not apply to Atal. 'What about his religious beliefs?' I feared that he might belong to some outlandish religious left wing. 'Atal is above all religions. He will surprise the world,' they said reverently.

I had seen some of his quotes in the local papers: 'If I am the right man, the party must be right too' and 'BJP will punish every corrupt congressman'. Also: 'What does Sonia know about poverty? I am the son of a poor schoolteacher.'

Sonia Gandhi (no relation to Mahatma Gandhi) was his closest rival. She was the widow of Rajvi Gandhi and a member of the Congress Party. Her mother-in-law, Indira Gandhi, was the daughter of Jawaharal Nehru, the first leader of India after Independence. She was not Indian-born but from a high-class Italian family.

In May 1998, less than three months after my conversation in the park, India proceeded with nuclear explosions in the Desert of Death. The Indian people were unabashedly jubilant. Pakistan instantly declared that it could match any step of nuclear escalation by India. A defiant India replied, 'Let the world know of India's capabilities. People will realise India is a strong nation and cannot be taken lightly.' So long trampled over by marauders from the north and Muslims from the west, this was India's big stick of defiance. Prime Minister Atal Behari Vajpayee was elected in February 1998 and again in October 1999.

I ventured into the subject of eating meat. 'It is dirty.' I looked carefully at them to see if they look skinny or malnourished. They didn't. They were on the lean side but looked healthy. It was another subject they seemed almost feverish to explain to me. 'To eat a cow would be like eating our mother. We cannot even think of it.'

'What is your age?' they asked me. Sometimes they were childlike in their directness. I didn't mind. 'I am 57.' I replied. They all fell back in surprise. They thought I was much younger. They asked if I ate meat. I wasn't shy about taking this increasingly rare gift of flattery and told them, 'Only a little.' 'Yes, yes, she's looking so young because she eats only little meat.' Little did they know I would have loved to know where I could get a good hunk of mother-cow in the form of a nice rare fillet steak.

When I asked why some of them spoke English and others didn't I learned the truth about education in Rajasthan. Everyone was entitled to go to school but there was such a shortage of schools that very few were lucky enough to have a place. The way to ensure a good education was to pay and few could afford more than a few years. Speaking English was

A Brush with India

a matter of how long they went to school. English was the second language but only if you had done at least six years at school. Few had that opportunity. They asked me to teach them a few phrases. 'Good afternoon. It is nice to meet you.' They were charming in their efforts, so willing and so good-natured. Naresh, one of the men who spoke English, taught me to say, 'Ram ram sa – hello, in the local dialect. I dutifully repeated it and everyone fell to the ground laughing. After an hour, I finally said goodbye. I hoped they found me as polite, generous in knowledge and as interesting as I found them.

Day nine and Gaston was worse. I stayed awake much of the night worrying about how I was going to get him home. A flight from Jodhpur to Delhi and then four more flights: Singapore, Bali, Brisbane and, finally, Auckland. I had nightmares about hiring helicopters and ambulances and trying to find someone who might change our tickets for a direct flight from Singapore to Auckland. Or could I just dump our tickets and pay for a one-way ticket? I knew it would cost more than our return flight but I didn't care about the money when health was involved. My thoughts went round in circles because I knew it was a hopeless idea. What airline was going to take him with a high fever and an enlarged heart? We could perhaps get away with it without saying anything but what if he had a heart attack?

Gaston repeatedly requested that I go out and try to enjoy myself because he only wanted to sleep. I ordered the car for nine in the morning: I had decided I would go to Umaid Palace – I had an idea that might help our situation.

As Meherangarh Palace dominates the skyline to the west, Umaid Bhawan Palace, sprawling over a low hill, dominates it to the east. Against the blue sky of the morning, the domes and towers signified the palace of a maharaja. Umaid Palace is not an old building: it was started in 1927 and finished by 1943. One of the worst famines known for many years occurred at that time and the palace's construction saved the lives of thousands of people by giving them employment. When the maharajas lost control of their individual kingdoms after Independence, many of them were forced to live off the income generated by converting their palaces into hotels. Grandiose is the best word to describe Umaid, a magnificent structure built

Jodhpur

of pink sandstone and marble brought in from local quarries. The entranceway and winding road up to its huge front gate was one of the few I had seen without potholes. The palace's huge kitchens and boiler rooms for heating and air conditioning proved to be ideal when it became a hotel. There is, on a lower floor, a large tiled swimming pool with cleverly concealed lighting. The floors are masterpieces of tiled designs. In the centre of the palace is a huge dome, seen as a landmark on the skyline for miles. Inside a fine winding marble staircase leads up to sumptuous rooms. In the museum, open to everyone, there are photos of some of the suites. They are like movie sets with their mirrored walls and marble floors, their black marble bathrooms and tiger-skin rugs. The room rate at Umaid Palace was well over US160, our hotel was only US20. The difference was hard to reconcile. Yesterday I watched a man eating from a garbage dump. Umaid Palace gave me a headache.

On the way back I asked Dinesh to stop at a hotel that I had seen earlier that day. I looked at a few of the rooms. Most had more sun than our present room, a fridge to keep drinks cold and bedside lights on both sides of the bed instead of just one in the middle. It was also cheaper. Though it was an ordeal for Gaston to move, we shifted over to the new place. The new surroundings were a good idea. Through the big window he could see the outline of Umaid Palace in the distance. Perhaps it was my imagination, but the beds did seem a little softer. I brought Gaston some soup and toast, the first food he had eaten for four days. Progress. He slept for the rest of the day, exhausted with the effort of moving, and his slumber seemed less disturbed.

In the late afternoon I went for a walk. The street was filled with antique shops: Jodhpur is a Mecca for antique hunters. Except for items over 100 years old there are no restrictions on buying and selling antiques and there seemed no end to what a person could purchase, from all types of religious items to what were obviously reproductions.

I didn't stop to have a good look. I needed to walk off my despair. I was once again the target of attention and although I wanted to be friendly I didn't want to get involved. Walking along in the dust, I constantly shook my head firmly at all the tuk-tuks that screamed to a halt at my side. I saw men squatting in the road, chipping away at marble slabs. Just, chip, chip, and chip all day long. I marvelled at their patience. I didn't even want to know how much they were paid. I was depressed enough.

Over my shoulder, I heard the words, 'Good afternoon, Ma'am. It is nice to see you.' It sounded so friendly that I decided to look. It was Naresh, the man I had met at the park the day before, cycling home from work. I yelled back, 'Ram ram sa!' and we had a good laugh. I felt an absolute wash of happiness at seeing someone I knew, be it ever so slightly. I explained we had changed hotels. He gave me his business card and we said goodbye.

On the way back I met a boy of about 10 who had formed a cricket team in an empty lot. Often the very first words an Indian will say to you are, 'Where are you from?' If it is a country that has been part of the British Empire and therefore plays cricket, they immediately follow with the name of the most famous cricket player from your country. So I was met with 'Richard Hadlee!' as the constant reply to 'New Zealand'. I must have heard that name a hundred times during my stay. Cricket is the game in India. In every schoolyard and every field someone has a bat and a ball and is fanatically playing that most British of games.

The next morning was our 10th day and at last Gaston was feeling better. He even felt up to a little sightseeing, so Dinesh and I took him up to Umaid Palace and then to the white marble memorial of Maharaja Jaswant Singh, opposite Meherangarh Fort. This is a grand spot to look over the entire city of Jodhpur, a peaceful place to contemplate this huge metropolis, and it offers an outstanding view of the fort.

Later in the afternoon we went for a quiet walk together. A few blocks from our hotel was the Ajit Bhawan Palace Hotel, the former residence of the last maharaja's brother. It was a delightful place with stone cottages, attractive gardens and a huge swimming pool. They also had tents, each containing a huge double bed, a lounge area and even a shower, toilet and washbasin. The floor was covered in thick and colourful Indian wool rugs, and the sides and ceiling were decorated with paintings of flowers and birds. But one look at the huge nets for the mosquitoes, and the knowledge that such a tent

Jodhpur

was twice the price of our present room, made us cool off our romantic ideas. There might be another time. We settled for a seat by the pool and a cold drink. I could hardly believe Gaston had improved so much in just one day and we did a lot of smiling at one another. He had lost a lot of weight: I could see it in his face. If a magic genie had come along at that moment and asked me for a wish I would have wanted to be instantly transported to our own garden. It was full summer now in New Zealand and the roses would be in bloom. I could have made dinner for Gaston, which he always prefers, and tucked him into his own king-size bed with its crisp sheets.

Later that night I was invited to an engagement party at the hotel. Hotel guests are sometimes invited to these occasions and are made overwhelmingly welcome. It was just as well that, before I sat down, I had noticed all the women guests sat on the left and the men on the right. I felt so conspicuous. Here I was again, a drab duck among swans. The women wore saris or shalwar khamiz (a long tunic top with trousers) in various shades of silk, satin and chiffon. Tiny beads, pearls and embroidery were scattered in beautiful designs on their clothing. With their long dark, rich brown hair, and their dusky brown eyes outlined in kohl, every one of them looked fascinatingly exotic. Indian women, even those who have never carried so much as a thimble on their heads, have a most elegant way of walking.

It was a shock, at first, to discover that most people living in India marry because of an arranged marriage. Although Hindus make up 82 per cent of the population, it is the custom in India for Sikhs, Jains, Muslims and even Christians to indulge in arranged marriages. In the main, the literature we read in the West portrays an arranged marriage as something bordering on barbaric, a loss of personal rights, but it is vitally important in the culture of India. The family is the core of life and in the rural villages that constitute most of the country's population, custom is the core of order. When there is a new wife to be added to the family, unity must be safeguarded. Family prosperity depends on the compatibility of the new couple and how well the wife can get on with her new family. The search for a wife can sometimes be a long one.

Qualities sought by both families are caste, status within

the caste, physical appearance (ideally lighter skinned), accomplishments, education, paid employment, hereditary birth defects such as diabetes and the financial status of the family. If there is mutual agreement that most of these things are suitable, the two families meet and enter negotiation. It is at this point that the bride and the groom meet for the first time or they may only be shown a photograph. If they absolutely cannot stand the sight of one another then that is usually accepted and the search continues. But once the two families agree the family astrologist is called in to study their horoscopes. If they are compatible, the betrothal takes place.

There are also a few other ways of making an arranged marriage. One is to advertise in the paper: the *Hindustan Times* of March 1998 had four full-length columns of 'brides wanted' advertisements. Some examples:

> 'WANTED charming punjabi girl for cultured family for smart 25 year old boy well settled in own Agra business, belonging small God fearing religious family'; 'WANTED A Beautiful Educated, Tall homely [in this case homely, meaning beautiful as the British interpret this word] girl for a very handsome boy, practicing chartered accountant. Monthly income in five figures. Biodata horoscope and photograph at first instance'; 'WANTED Green Card Holder Bride alone independent Agarwal doctor, vegetarian never married, Hindi speaking, willing to settle abroad, caste no bar, divorcee/widow also considerations'; 'DELPHITE Match must be a convent girl, very pretty, first class law graduate girl who will practice simultaneously dedicating herself ideally to household duties. Father first class officer, well settled advocates preferred.'

There were similar advertisements seeking bridegrooms. Unlike our personal and dating ads, these suitors didn't mention personal interests. For instance, there wasn't one that said he/she liked music, or dancing, or running or theatre. It seems calculated but when a girl goes into a new family, her mother-in-law is number one and she becomes number two or even three on the totem pole. Her mother-in-law will be giving the orders and the new bride must learn to fit into the order of things.

The third way of finding a partner is the matrimonial agencies. They charge a fee and, instead of being approached by suitors, it is the parents of the boy or girl who seek their services. Families are introduced to families: it is a union between two families rather than just the two people.

The fourth way is self-choice, which is labelled a 'love-marriage'. It is becoming more popular, but usually only in the large cities. For most of the population it is frowned upon.

If everyone is happy and the horoscopes are compatible, arrangements for the wedding can go ahead. A dowry is illegal but almost inevitably some sort of financial agreement is made. An auspicious day is found and the priest selected. Weddings occur from December through to July. (Because of the monsoon, August through November are not good months for festivities). The wedding takes place at the bride's home and all expenses are paid for by the father, including hiring a hall if necessary and paying for caterers. The bride's parents give her gold ornaments such as necklaces, bangles and rings.

At the hotel I had been told this was not a wedding but an engagement party: the bride and groom would meet for the first time and go through certain rituals. The bride, aged about 20, was dressed in a red sari with gold borders. The groom looked a little older. They were both very handsome. I watched them closely. They never looked at one another, even though they were sitting side by side in red velvet chairs. She, in particular, never smiled or showed any emotion. I thought it entirely possible she didn't like him. The service was in Hindi. When I was asked to leave my chair I suddenly felt embarrassed, thinking I had somehow done the wrong thing, but I was brought up to the front so I could see well. Anita, the sister of the bride, looking exquisite in soft champagne satin, had taken me under her wing. Everyone treated me as an honoured guest and talked to me at once. The bride, groom and I were the stars. I wondered what I should do next. There were expensive cameras everywhere: this was obviously a very wealthy family. Before I knew what was happening, I was placed between the prospective bride and groom and my photo was taken. There were 200 guests and I felt overwhelmed by their attention, their generosity. The children, also dressed immaculately, were the most well-mannered I have ever met. Nerendra, an outstandingly handsome boy of 12, told me in perfect English, 'Anything you want is my wish and everyone else's as well.' I must take sweets. I must have cake to celebrate the occasion. Would I like a Pepsi? Please, please, please, could I stay for dinner? (I had already eaten.) I still had my eye on the bride and groom. Finally, I saw her glance at him and a tiny smile appeared at her lips. As for him, he looked like a man on the threshold of a very fine and enjoyable life. Anita told me they would not see each other until November, eight months away, when the wedding took place. Could I please, please come? It would mean so much. I took dozens of photos, which I eventually mailed back to them, but I left early. I felt it was their party and I didn't want to take any further attention away from the others. The children, dozens of them, followed me back to our room and Gaston got up to say hello. They fell over him as if he was some sort of god. We said goodnight and closed the door. I lay awake for a long time thinking surprisingly favorable things about arranged marriages.

Our last day in Jodhpur; tomorrow we would leave for Ajmer and Pushkar. We had come all this way and Gaston had been unable to work. I took several rolls of film in case he could use some for painting, but he almost never does. His entire emphasis is about colour and light, which cannot come from a photograph. Sometimes he can manage a watercolour from a photograph but prefers not to. It was not surprising that he was feeling depressed about progress. If the single painting he did in Jaisalmer was sold, his share of the proceeds, less commission, taxes and cost of framing, wouldn't be anywhere near enough to justify this jaunt in the desert. It had been great for me, as there was such a lot to see and think about, but Gaston's whole reason for being in India was to produce paintings for his next major exhibition in 14 months. If the majority were not finished now, we would need to make another expensive overseas trip.

I am often asked if there are some paintings that I want to keep. I would like to keep every one of them. They are all memories of our life and they probably mean more to me then anyone else. If I am lucky enough to keep one, it never leaves our house. Clients have come to us and offered excellent money for paintings hanging in our living room. Many were sold and I finally said, 'Never again.' Money comes and mostly goes but our paintings are windows on our life together. To me, it is like selling a love letter. For exhibitions, they all must be for sale. If we were to take one or two to keep for ourselves, it would diminish the overall impact. A professional artist cannot afford to keep his work: paintings on our walls do not pay the bills. It is a consolation to occasionally see a favourite painting in another home: knowing where it is and knowing that people love it makes me feel content.

There is never any guarantee that a painting will sell. Some subjects sell more quickly than others. In Gaston's case, street scenes and marketplaces are always good but they should be European. I silently pick my favourites in an exhibition. In the last, my pick was the last to sell. Over the years I have learnt the hard way to keep my mouth zipped.

A return to Meherangarh Fort seemed a great idea for our last day. Gaston was well enough this time to make the long climb up to the palace, though we took it in easy stages. At the top, warmed by the walk, we sat in large padded cane chairs at the restaurant, drinking coffee in the sun and watching some Indian VIPs at the tables next to us. The waiters slavishly gave a flourish of bows and wide smiles. The most important, a politician of course, wore a white cotton high-collared shirt, white trousers and a brown sleeveless jacket and sandals. His appearance was stately but ostensibly humble, rather like the sparkle from a tiny two-carat diamond. At any moment, I expected him to reach out, lay a hand on someone's head and say the Hindi equivalent of 'Bless you, my son'. Everyone gathered around him, pressing their palms together and upwards in endless greetings and namastes, hoping for some response. They got very little, except a rather tight smile. It seems an odd contradiction that, in India, politicians of unquestionable wealth wear clothing only a few steps away from the plain white dhoti of the great and genuinely humble Gandhi. Our own politicians in the West, so strikingly different, strut around in their designer suits, Cardin shirts, shiny shoes and wide smiles.

We felt mellow and happy again. 'For once,' I said, trying

to make things easier, 'why can't we just have a vacation and walk around and enjoy things?' He agreed. I knew it won't last but at the moment it felt right.

We went to the top of the fort where he experienced, as I had, the wonder of the sound of a million people: a cacophony, a babble, a din, a tumult of voices, a chest tightener, a heart stopper, an eye widener; the rhythm of life in full panoramic sound and Technicolor. It was magnificent. It was harrowing.

On the way down the steep descent, we came across the same little girl I had seen the first time I went to Meherangarh Fort. The sensuous music, played by the father, started as soon as we approached and the girl began to dance. To my astonishment, as soon as she began, Gaston ran behind a wall. The music and the dancing stopped. The father looked puzzled. Out Gaston came again and, looking her straight in the eye, advanced toward her. More music, more dancing. He disappeared behind another wall. I was cringing with embarrassment. What was he doing? After three or four repetitions, I heard the sweetest sound: the little girl was laughing. She was having fun with this stranger who was playing silly games with her. All day long, people thrust cameras in her face or videoed her little body, but here was someone who made her giggle. He stole her heart. Mine too.

Back at the parking lot I could see the little shoeshine boy who had wanted to polish my sandals a few days ago. The other pedlars were there, the spice merchants with their signs blazed in large letters: teas, curry powder, fruit, spices, tandori, Indian marsala, garam marsala, saffron (zafran), cardamom, cinnamon, nutmeg, ginger, coriander, poppy seeds, asafetida, sesame, paprika. The little plastic bags seemed endless and the spiel: 'You must buy. Why won't you buy? I give you best price!' But it was the little boy who had my attention. We were old friends now. We talked as best we could. Last time I had given him 20 rupees. This time he drew me down and whispered in my ear, so the others could not hear, 'Please, give me 100 rupees, I need to buy many chapatis.' I knew then that the Shoe-Shine Kid was going to be all right.

Chapter 5
Ajmer and Pushkar

AFTER A LONG, HOT AND tiring trip of 235 kilometres, (145 miles) we finally turned off the main road and drove into Ajmer which, for most people, is just a town you must pass through to get to Pushkar. But for Moslems, it is a major religious centre and an important place of pilgrimage during the fast of Ramadan. The Moslem order known as Sufi reveres the city as the burial place of their saint, Khwaja Muin-ud-din Chishti.

The two main religions, Hindu and Islam, have been the essence of daily life and politics in India for the last 1000 years. Three years before the turn of the first millennium the Moslem invader Sultan Mahmed crossed into Hindustan. By AD1200, Moslem sultans had established their capital in Delhi. The foundation of the Mogul Empire had started by 1526, ending at the beginning of the 1700s. The reason so few Moslems could make so many Hindus subservient, was not due to the indifference of the Indian people. It was the result of their non-assertive religion, Hinduism, and a non-allied population, which was continually disturbed and divided by outside invaders.

When the Moslem conquerors first came to India, their priority was to take back to their own country as much booty as they could carry. The Moslem warriors considered all disbelievers, such as the Hindus, to be heretics and heathens. In their eyes, to utterly destroy centuries old, irreplaceable Hindu temples was a positive victory for Allah. It wasn't long before the victors wanted territory as well as treasure. Over the successive years, they managed to confiscate and rule as far south as the Deccan, nearly halfway down the Indian continent. Vast and powerful Mogul kingdoms, which made England look like a cow-cocky 10-acre farm, took residence and control. But although the Hindu religion may have been repressed for nearly 700 years, it never died out. The Hindu people did, however, suffer agonising humiliation, financial ruin and inhuman brutality. The new Moslem regime created so strong a hatred for Islam that Hindu beliefs became the hidden soul of India, their invisible raft of survival. The descendants of these two religions are the constant sources of hate, division and suspicion.

When the British came on the scene they managed to subdue some of the bitter feelings between the two religious groups. Although there was a certain amount of distrust it was also a time of learning to live with one another. The biggest problem for the Moslems was that, when the British took control, they became a minority and were no longer in power. The Hindu religion accounted for a whopping 80 per cent of the population. Under the British, Hindu culture and the idea and hope for a united India began to regenerate. The Hindus took to the technology, the learning institutions and administration processes, albeit British, with a fever only the long suppressed can comprehend. The Moslems, on the other hand, stood aside, thinking that Allah would provide and perhaps bring back some of their old glory. The old adage 'God helps those who help themselves' was perhaps never more poignant.

Gandhi understood the Moslems. He knew that separating Hindus and Moslems and making them two nations would not solve India's problems and would certainly lead to more and more violence. Moslems believe that religion and affairs of the state are inseparable. Owing to their loss of leadership, and with the impending new government and its overwhelming Hindu representation, Moslem insecurity became the reason for the nation of Pakistan. When India became an independent nation in August 1947, the six weeks that followed were a bloody and savage confrontation. In that short span of time, half as many Indians would lose their lives as the total number of Americans who died in the Second World War. Pakistan, for the Moslem people, was only a triumph of religion: it had no infrastructure and no political substance. Mohammad Ali Jinnah, the first prime minister and the man responsible for making Pakistan a reality, died within months of taking office. India has gone from strength to strength but Pakistan has not developed a modern economy and corruption has become so deep it is almost impossible to control.

Ajmer and Pushkar

It was impossible for Pakistan to absorb all the Moslems of India: more remained in India than were to move to Pakistan. The Moslems who chose to stay in India were left in a tenuous and touchy position. Almost every Indian, be they Moslem, Sikh, Parsee or Hindu, lost family and loved ones during the time of partition. The wounds, on all sides, are still fresh.

Ajmer is a city of nearly a half million people and our impression was that it was the dirtiest city we had seen. We drove slowly because the streets were a foot deep in foul, dark water. Piled high on the roadside were large, black mounds of rags, wadded paper and sewage. Filthy sludge squelched and spurted under our tyres. Traffic problems were oppressive, abetted by languid cows, odorous goats, wild-eyed dogs and hairy herds of roving pigs; even the animals were in a bad state.

Ajmer is home to Mayo College, the famous primary and secondary school established by the British in 1875. The first students arrived by elephant, complete with an entourage of servants, camels and anything else a young maharaja might need. In its early years this school was a place of education entirely for the sons of Indian aristocracy. Students came from families so wealthy that entire houses were built for their children while they attended college. Based on the English public school system, Mayo was considered the Eton of the East. Once the young prince left he was expected to continue on to Oxford or Cambridge. Mayo is still one of the most prestigious schools in India. Although a new girls' wing was introduced 10 years ago, the main school for girls in Ajmer is the illustrious Sophia College. Previously, wealthy families often sent their daughters to what were originally convents in Ajmer. Now they are more likely to be called finishing schools. But, even today, in the marriage columns, it is common to see the request for a girl from a convent school.

Dinesh was in a hurry to leave the largely Moslem town of Ajmer and we drove on to the holy city of Pushkar, only 11 kilometres (7 miles) away over a small mountain pass called Nag Pahar, or Snake Mountain. For the first time since our visit to Rajasthan, we saw large roving bands of Langur monkeys. They sat on the roadside, grinding their long sharp teeth together, snapping their mouths open and shut, like

A Brush with India

hungry, ill-paid guards sizing up the newcomers for food and ways to make mischief. I had learnt the hard way about wild monkeys, a few weeks earlier in Bali. Monkeys can be dangerous. If they think you have food and they want it, they will cling to your legs, arms or whatever they can get a hold of and flash their teeth. They do bite.

Pushkar is a surprisingly small town with a population of only 12,000. It has a small lake at its centre with white houses and ghats built around it. Travellers come to this holy city for rest and relaxation, usually after being on the road for a long time. It has a world famous annual camel fair. Perhaps more importantly, it is a place of pilgrimage that should be visited by a Hindu once in his lifetime.

Pushkar is the only place where Hindus can come and worship their highly important god, the lord of creation, Brahma. The lake, according to the story, appeared after Brahma dropped a lotus flower from the heavens, though no one knows exactly when. One day, Brahma decided to go to the lake at Pushkar, to perform a sacrifice. For reasons known only to him, but in a familiar scenario, he took with him a 'companion', the beautiful Gayatra. His jealous wife Savitri found out and was neither amused nor happy. Feeling betrayed, she made a deal with the gods that Brahma could not be worshipped anywhere but Pushkar. So Hindus must come to Pushkar.

The Hindu religion is not easy to understand: it is a huge basket of ideas that have been added to over an extremely long time. Hardly anything has been removed or changed. The proprietors of the basket felt there was room for every idea and god, as long as they were positive for their personal agenda. Hinduism is, like many religions, a type of control to regulate and formulate a civilisation. It evolved to give order to races, languages, occupations, religious practices and geographical areas.

Caste was one way of bringing about control, position and possession. Called The Laws of Manu, it was a way of grading and segregating men. Those who were at the top made sure they stayed that way, kept or added to what they had and organised a workforce that would look after them. There were and are 7000 castes made up from four major castes.

The highest were the Brahmans, whose lifetime purpose is to teach and to study the Vedas (Hindu scriptures). They were the priests of the Hindu religion and the men who performed sacrifices. The second highest were the Kshatriyas, who were the kings and warriors. (Many Rajputs were Kshatriyas.) Their job was to protect and look after the people and to study the Vedas. The third group were the Vaishyns, the farmers, merchants, cattle breeders, tillers of the soil, moneylenders, traders and so on. They were to go about their daily work and study the Vedas. The last group were the Shudras, also known as Harijans, Untouchables or the Unscheduled. They were not a caste as such, but servants to all the others. They were never to study the Vedas. One can never change one's caste and intermarriage is not acceptable.

The Hindu religion is based upon the concept that a succession of reincarnations is necessary to achieve moksha, the state that finally releases a person from the cycle of rebirth. Karma is the factor or law of cause and effect. The universe is a harmonious whole only when nature, gods and men fulfil their prescribed sets of duties. For example, the seasons, the weather and the tides must do what they normally do. The gods must also do their duty and be willing to come to humankind's aid. And humans must perform and follow the customs of the groups they are born in. Every act of life, no matter how trivial, is a religious ritual and a prescribed obligation. Personal identity has nothing to do with it.

Remarkably, Hinduism has managed to blend the countless (somewhere near three million) cults and gods of India from its many ages and differing people into one vast mythology, a gargantuan basket of idols. The main gods, the big three, are Brahma the creator, Shiva the destroyer and Vishnu the preserver. The other gods include ancient and new, sacred and epic, animals, birds, mountains, rivers and plants. Many of these can also be avatars, reincarnations of themselves in different forms. Also there are individual gods assigned to help in specific tasks: for example, Ganesha, the elephant-headed god who can assure success, or Kali, Hinduism's most frightening goddess, who may find a way of making a barren woman pregnant.

Hinduism is an ancient religion handed down from century

to century. It is close up and personal, devout and practised. Each house has its own area for daily prayer and meditation. Today, the people of different castes are slowly becoming more understanding and tolerant of each other: the caste system survives but it is changing. But the old values and love for Hinduism are still strong and important in all phases of Indian life. In Pushkar strict rules apply to everyone. Alcohol, meat and eggs are forbidden. Drugs are strictly prohibited and anyone caught using them faces serious penalties. As it is a holy place, no hand holding or other signs of affection, such as kissing, are allowed. One should also refrain from smoking.

The date of Pushkari's spectacular camel fair held sometime in November, depends on the full moon and the timing is important, for the cleansing of sins by bathing in the lake at exactly the propitious date is vital. People from all over the world come to India to see this fair. Camels, those powerhouses of agriculture, commerce and transport, are admired and judged for both strength and beauty. Fifty thousand animals make their way through the pass at Snake Mountain, and crowds of more than 100,000 come to watch thousands of tribespeople conducting the serious business of buying and selling their camels. Women in brightly coloured saris and heavy jewellery, men in white dhotis and coloured turbans mingle with the tourists. Enormous, self-contained tent cities are erected to accommodate the deluge of people, local and foreign. But it is not all camel bartering; it is also a time of festivities with street entertainers, musicians, contests and camel races, and street stalls at their best.

We drove through the impossibly narrow streets looking for a hotel. On the way I took photos from the car window of a snake charmer, a Kalbelia. The sound of the poongi, the traditional snake charmer's flute, filled the air as the flat silver head of a cobra rose from its small basket. I snapped away while we drove past and the snake charmer raised his fist at me. I had not thought about tossing him money and realised that I had made a bumbling mistake. I should have given him something: a snake charmer belongs to a particular caste and this was his main source of earning a living, possible his only income.

The Pushkar palace hotel is the most popular and luxurious

place to stay in Pushkar. Since Gaston had such a difficult time, we decided to stay at more comfortable accommodation while he was convalescing. The best rooms were reasonably priced: that was the good news. The bad news was they didn't have any vacant rooms, but they could give us a tent: I was going to get my wish and stay in a desert tent. Dinesh, who was allowed to stay on the roof in a dorm tent, seemed as happy about his accommodation as I was about our tent.

The ceiling of our new canvas abode was made up of 16 alternating triangular panels of green and blue. The floor was covered in layers of thick green carpets piled on top of each other. The walls were painted in bouquets of flowers. We had a table, two chairs, a bench for our luggage and a large double bed made up with the inevitable two single beds joined with a large sheet. Thick, warm-looking eiderdowns encased in thin gauze sheets were our separate covers. There was electricity and an excellent heater. We had everything we needed except a toilet and a handbasin, which were a short walk down the corridor. The hotel had excellent management who told us repeatedly whatever we wished was their only desire. Tomorrow, they assured us, they would have an 'excellent, very excellent room' for us. We felt as if we were following the butler as he showed us the dining room where a nightly buffet was served. Would we care to sit in the cane chairs, relax in the sun, look at the peaceful lake and have a cold drink? Non alcoholic, of course. Would we like to be in luxurious surroundings, and pretend to be idle rich tourists, just for once? Oh, yes. Oh, yes.

Arriving at the hotel we noticed several well-dressed men milling around handing out flowers. Speaking quietly, they suggested that when we went down to the lake we should toss the flowers into the water. 'It will bring good luck,' they insisted. 'We will go with you.' Now I knew for sure that no one was going to be hanging around hotels handing out flowers just to bring me good luck. What was it all about? It wouldn't be long before we found out.

At five o'clock Dinesh met us to go out searching for possible painting sites. We could not drive through the centre of Pushkar. The streets were narrow, many were blocked off and it was impossible for two cars to negotiate the constricted

A Brush with India

lanes. Skirting the town and arriving at the other end, we decided to leave the car and walk back. Dinesh was frowning at us again and gave us an extra stern warning not to talk to anyone. It would have helped if he had explained what to expect.

As we got out of the car, a crowd of handsome, young, flower-bearing men descended upon us. They purred, 'We do not want anything. We are only humble priests who wish to be of service to you.' Priests? So many? Why do we need priests? It was too obvious that we were foreigners. Furious with their constant approaches and patter, Gaston pushed past, while I was left smiling foolishly, trying to catch up with him. We continued our walk through the streets. Our main objective was to get near the ghats (stairs) leading down into the lake. Clue number one: we found out that any blue painted wall means it is a holy place. Blue is the sacred colour of Brahma. Whenever you see a painting or picture with a rather handsome blue man, this is your guy. Clue number two: you need a passport to proceed. You need a what?

No sooner had we turned into our first blue-walled alley than a young man bearing flowers accosted us yet again. This time I had to find out what this was leading to, so I let myself be guided halfway down the steps to the lake. My new friend was giving me a long spiel, something about Brahma and monks. He lifted my hands, put them together to form a bowl and then filled them with bright orange marigolds. He was too handsome, too young, too slick. I remembered reading that Pushkar was full of priests and that not all of them were bona fide. If I was going to need a passport, it was going to have to come from someone who at least looked like a priest. He flinched and looked a little startled as I dumped the flowers into his hands and rushed back up the stairs. Gaston, of course, had wisely retreated into the streets long before.

The only way we were going to find out if the lake was suitable as a painting subject was to somehow get down to it. This time we approached the blue walls furtively, looking for an opening, a small passage that might not be holy ground. We almost made it. We were halfway down when an elderly man with a long beard and wearing a dhoti asked if we needed some help. First, we checked him out for flowers. Nada.

'Would we be allowed to photograph the lake?'

'Yes, of course, that would be perfectly acceptable.' His head nodded from right to left and back again. 'Come, come, I am taking you all the way down to the water. I am so happy to show you the holy place of Brahma.'

We walked further and suddenly, through an arched blue portal, the lake came into full view. 'I will be giving you the holy blessing of Brahma,' he said. We started to back away. 'No, no, it is my honour. I am very happy to be giving you.' He looked the part anyway.

I decided I wanted to find out, finally, what this was all about. So with courage on my part, and flowers and a coconut in the hands of the priest, the two of us went down to the last step and the edge of the lake. The ringing of temple bells and the softer sounds of wind chimes filled the air. The smell of incense drifted and settled like a blue ghost on our shoulders. The sacred mantra, 'Asvodityow Brahma', was repeated over and over. It was so unlike anything I had ever known or experienced. I knew only that the lake was a sacred place. I was trying to comprehend what was happening, without prejudice. The blessing was nearly all in Hindi so I couldn't understand a word. All that was left for me was to look interested, and hope for 'enlightenment'. Water was poured through my hands. I dutifully repeated after him, 'The sun is Brahma, the sun is Brahma.' He blessed my children. He asked their names. He blessed my grandchildren. And in particular he blessed my husband who was watching us from a far too respectful distance.

At some point in the blessing, among all the Hindi, I heard some quite clear English words that hinted I might like to give 500 rupees, maybe 200, to the priests: 'No problem how much'. I suggested perhaps 10. He completely ignored my suggestion. I kept repeating the sacred vows in copycat Hindi. I sounded ridiculous. Soon we had gone through the entire genealogy of my family. We dipped our hands in red powder and touched it to our foreheads. We threw flowers into the water. We slowly and ceremoniously passed the coconut in circles. The priest lifted water from the lake and splashed it on my hair. I was at last ready to receive my passport to Pushkar. The priest lifted my hand. A piece of string, red and yellow twined together, was tied around my wrist. I was now blessed. We walked reverently up the steps. Gaston, flat against the wall, unable to get any further back, was also blessed with a red dot of powder, a tika, to his forehead. After so much effort, how could we not be convinced that 50 rupees for Brahma and 50 rupees for the priest would not be the right thing to do? It was a blessing all right – once I had that little precious piece of string around my wrist the flower men left us completely alone.

We felt more settled now that we knew the secret of the blue walls. We strolled through the city, relaxed and keen to look at the souvenirs and knick-knacks of Pushkar. There was really nothing we wanted to buy. We stopped at a hole in the wall that was the abode of a moneychanger and refused his comic first offering for our American dollars. We went through the usual two-step vocal prance, forward a little, back a little. The final hurrah was our usual one, 'Goodbye, we will exchange our money at the hotel.' To which his final performance was, 'I will match the hotel.' Well, not exactly his final capitulation: he first had to short-change us, coming up with the excuse he was just going to get some more money.

We walked through the streets. There were the usual tourist items for sale – bottles of mineral water, silver jewellery, cotton skirts, shirts and toilet paper of the thinnest quality – which all had a look of sad abandonment, like pets at the SPCA. At some stalls we saw spectacular mounds of red, blue, yellow and green powder, used for religious ceremonies. Peaked into volcano shapes, little balls of colour occasionally ran down the sides. Like a jumbo box of crayons, new and pristine, they were jewel-like in their intensity.

It was in Pushkar that I discovered a real bargain that can be bought all over India: recorded music, CDs and tapes, from classical to pop, including an overwhelming array of Indian music. Most sell for about half the price of their equivalents in Western countries.

Indian music is completely different from European music. To comprehend it, it is necessary to understand that the Indian musical scale is based on 22 quarter tones, not the 12 tones we use. According to legend, these notes were created from the cries of the peacock, cow, goat, heron, nightingale, horse and elephant. Peacock calls, like those of nightingales, are unchangeable in pitch but the other five can be sharp or flat notes. There are also variations, which produce approximately 22 tones. Like most things Indian, the creation of Indian music is an extension of their religious philosophy. Sounds are considered the disintegration of one world note, the voice of God. An orchestra is provided not for enjoyment as an orchestra but as an accompaniment for a singer or for a solo instrumentalist.

Ragas (themes) consist of at least 72 classical melodies and 800, perhaps more, are derived from each of the main themes. The soloist starts out with a raga developed from one of the main themes and infinite variations of that theme develop, depending on the passion of the soloist. As Europeans we are not familiar with classical Indian themes and our untrained ear cannot understand the fine nuances of improvisation. Except in the field of jazz, we are not accustomed to extemporised melodies: unaccustomed to the fine changes of the tune, we tend to hear a repetitive sound. It might be compared to reading a book with neither full stops nor paragraphs. Unless you have grown up with this system it is hard to follow and 'thoughts' or melodies all run together and sound the same.

Later that night we tried the buffet at the hotel. Eating had become an obsession for us. We had still not adjusted to the highly spiced food and the lack of something solid to get our teeth into. The restaurant had a nice ambience with its polished wooden tables and flickering candles. Placed here and there were antique chests and armoires. Polished copper pans and old woven carpets hung on the walls. The staff welcomed us as if we were part of their family. The dinner was the best we had since we left Bikaner. Recognisable and refreshing, the warm tomato soup served with fresh chapatis was a balm to our stomachs. And although there was no meat, the three vegetables – potatoes, cauliflower and spinach – served in their individual sauces were cooked and seasoned to perfection. Rice and freshly sliced cabbage, tomatoes and onions gave colour and pleasure to our eyes. A mouth-watering rice pudding appeared for dessert. As we enjoyed our meal, we began to relax. At last we were in a place where we could begin again and perhaps Gaston could get some work done.

We looked forward to our first night in our tent. The bed was good, our blankets were clean and warm and coming from the lake was the unmistakable sound of exotic Indian music. Later, stretched out in the dark we held hands and listened to drums and a male voice, singing insistently, powerfully. It was strange and mysterious. It was wonderful. It was wonderful for about an hour. An unfamiliar rhythm and a strange repetitive voice in a language we couldn't comprehend gradually became tedious. Then it became unbearable. The hours collapsed into each other and the music continued on. The same notes changed in moods, a little angry, a little passionate, a little pleading, but always the same basic sound. After five hours, we were still awake. At 4 a.m. it stopped. Peace. One hour later the cacophony started again. This time it was the wail of a woman singing what sounded like a love song. At 5.30 the monks from the temple across the lake began their morning pujas, with the sound of prayers, bell ringing and cymbal clashing. To complete the trio, the indisputable chant of a group of Hari Krishnas added their familiar droning.

We packed our bags in silence. We allowed the memory of the dreamlike quality of the lake and the good food, which gave us back our joy in eating, linger for a moment and let it slide away. The mosquitoes, the floundering in the dark corridors to find the toilet and, above all, the music that continued long after sufferance had given way to steely endurance, made staying impossible.

Dinesh was thrilled we were leaving. He, too, had had no sleep and had been uneasy since our arrival. He seemed unusually impatient to leave. To get back to the main highway took more than an hour. Gaston was convinced we were on the wrong road.

Chapter 6

Jaipur and Bharatpur, Keoladeo National Park

WE HAD EXPERIENCED THE highway to hell. We thought the roads in South America were the worst, but now they were relegated to second place. The 235 kilometre (142 mile) highway between Ajmer and Jaipur is also part of the main highway between Delhi and the seaport of Bombay. Don't make this journey by car. Unless you have just completed a climbing trip to the Himalayas and have become totally desensitised by near-death experiences, make haste to the nearest airport or railway station instead. Seventy thousand people die every year as a result of road accidents in India. The axiom to remember at all times is: might is right. The larger the vehicle, the more right it has to the road. Evasion at all times is the rule. Get out of the way or prepare for your next life. Driving is supposed to be on the left-hand side, like the British, but more than likely it is done, wherever possible, in the middle of the road, to avoid potholes and permit maximum speed.

Every truck in India has 'HORN PLEASE' written in large letters on the back. It doesn't take long to understand what this means: honk like hell if you want to pass and if you value your life at all. There were so many trucks on the road that I had to count them. It turned out to be 11 trucks per minute, about 660 trucks per hour, in one lane. This total didn't include private cars, camels, bullocks and carts, or motorbikes. Describing the road as a two-lane highway was vastly generous: one and three-quarters was more like it and only when it wasn't under construction. Then, it was one driving lane and one rock and boulder lane.

The construction workers, hardworking women in saris, carried road materials in large woven baskets on their heads. They tiptoed through black boiling pitch, depositing rocks

A Brush with India

and medium-sized boulders, as daintily as if they were in a field of daisies. Twelve-year-old boys lifted buckets of fiery tar, threaded through bamboo poles, and dumped the boiling contents onto the rocks. Road maintenance continued, directly alongside these women and children, with extremely dense traffic travelling at maximum speed.

Tata is the manufacturer of most trucks in India, which were the moving tin-can monsters of the desert. The roof of our little Ambassador car was one-third the height of these awesome giants. Not only were they high but also obscenely overloaded. It was hard to understand the logic but these trucks were licensed to carry 25 per cent more than the manufacturer suggested as safe. They always leaned to one side – ours. On the rare times we passed a Tata we felt as if we were zooming under verandahs. If there was a delay, there was no such thing as just waiting until the hold-up was cleared. No, Tata monsters always needed to 'move 'em out' – out into your lane, out into the desert, out into anything as long as they kept going. If the driver could pass the truck in front of him on the left instead of the right, this was great truck one-upmanship. As they whizzed past, we could see decorative paintings of birds, cows and flowers on the sides. At the front and back Christmas tree ornaments jiggled up and down, sparkling in the sun. When a truck slowed we could even make out the evil eye paintings and read some elegantly penned prose such as 'Even you of the evil eye, may God bless you,' or 'Use dipper at night and wait for hand waving'. The one with the really relevant ring was, 'Regard the world with love, and remember you take nothing with you when you die.'

I rode shotgun in the front while Gaston brought up the rear. I needed to see properly because I was going to get out and kill the next guy who passed us just one more time, too close and too fast. Gaston, full of antibiotics and an elixir of god-knows-what was lying down with his face toward the back of the seat.

We passed a dozen wrecked Tatas lying on their sides. There were often two trucks, the result of head-on collisions. Cargos removed, bodies disentangled, they lay prostrate and abandoned. There was no way, and no reason, to remove such battered mountains of metal out on the highway.

Jaipur and Bharatpur, Keoladeo National Park

Mangled mammoths, with metal dinosaur-like bones, that wouldn't decay or rust in the desert, they remained as silent advertisements of grisly roadside tales.

I could see it coming. It's funny how it really is in slow motion when these things happen, as if the mind desperately looks for its own brakes. To our right, in the opposite lane, a big Tata rammed hard into the back of the truck in front of him. There was a shudder of steel against steel, the noise ramming deep into our ears. A huge spray of glass followed, with shooting semi-circles of sparkling prisms of light. Then silence. Then red, red blood on an open-mouthed face. We dared not stop. The other lane would build up into a nightmare back-up of miles of waiting vehicles. We kept going to so that one lane at least would remain open.

The journey seemed endless. We saw the old remnants of another wreck. A passenger bus lay on its side down a short bank. This time a truck had ploughed into the centre of a passenger bus, no doubt overloaded with human cargo. A few minutes later we nearly had a collision ourselves, when a giant horned animal came hurtling out of the bush straight in front of us. Shocked, breathless from the sight of the animal inches from my face, unable to speak, I looked at Dinesh. He, rather casually, said, 'It was a blackbuck.'

By the time we were near Jaipur we were wrung out from fatigue and tight nerves. I understood why Dinesh's mother didn't want him to be a driver. It is of enormous credit to the commercial drivers of India that they manage to negotiate such difficult and dangerous roads. Construction and maintenance are nightmares. In winter at 25°C (78°F) it is wretched; in summer with temperatures approaching 50°C (120°F) it is life-threatening. The whole scenario is a testimony to desperation and an agreement to survive at any cost.

The wonderful thing about having a driver and a car was not having to trudge around with luggage in hand when looking for a place to stay. If we didn't like what we saw we just drove on to the next place. By the time we arrived in Jaipur, however, we were in no mood to shop around. We took the first place, the Madhuban Guest House. The gods must have directed us, perhaps in a generous mood of amusement and appeasement, after our nightmare drive: the room turned out to be one of our best yet. It was reasonably priced, spotlessly clean and, for the first time, we had a normal double bed with normal double sheets and blankets.

A brilliant young Bengali architect built Jaipur in 1725. It was a city designed with the palace at its heart, and that palace had to be a big one because Maharaja Jai Singh, warrior-architect-astronomer, had 28 wives and several hundred concubines. Unlike other Indian towns that grew like untamed weeds, Jaipur flowed outwards into an amazingly well planned grid system, with wide streets and boulevards. A fortified wall containing seven gates encircled the entire city. Three hundred years ago, when Jaipur was built, the main risks were invading armies and marauding animals that inhabited the surrounding forest. It was hard to imagine it now. There were no surrounding forests; the animals were few and confined to reserves; as for invading armies, they came on tourist buses.

They called it the Pink City because it was given a pink wash in 1876 – for the visit of the Prince of Wales: pink signified hospitality – this colour has been maintained by law, until this day. Its beauty is not readily apparent at first glance, but it is a remarkable place, built before the Boston Tea Party and the Declaration of Independence, before Cook explored the Pacific and even when the Persians were still pillaging Delhi.

By 1950, the population of Jaipur was 300,000; now it is edging towards 2 million. As with the towns of ancient Greece, most of the original city walls have disappeared for building purposes. Besides the population explosion, the weather exacerbates the living problems and evaporates the water supply. Jaipur has an annual rainfall of only 64 millilitres and summer temperatures with an average of more than 40°C(100°F). In 1998, Jaipur had several days of heat over 50°C(120°F). The time to visit, therefore, is between September and March, winter to spring.

Jaipur may not be as beautiful as it once was but makes up for this by its bristling energy and life. In the morning and afternoon, bicycle rickshaws were more numerous then cars. Many were overflowing with school children, sometimes seven or eight at a time: it was hard to figure out how one human being could pull so many kids. Dressed in school uniforms, the girls had braided, raven hair held with ribbons and the boys white shirts firmly tucked in. They looked so implausibly neat and tidy in the heat and the bustle. Many carried stainless steel, multi-tiered tiffin carriers, the Indian equivalent of school lunch boxes. They laughed, chatted, ate sweets and snobbishly ignored the rickshaw driver with his hunched shoulders and bare callused feet. To be the regular driver for a family, to have the contract to deliver children to school every day, is only an unobtainable dream for most.

On street corners and sometimes whole blocks, large groups of people made the pavement their homes. They were blacksmiths, called Gaduliya Lohars, descendants from an ancient tribe of the Rajputs. Their former specialty was as providers of munitions to the rulers of Rajasthan, royal outfitters of warfare; now they repaired pots and pans. Displaced by Akbar the Mogul king 400 years ago, they were now nomadic. Walking in the street was difficult because it was necessary to circumnavigate their beds and crude shelters of old pieces of plastic and cardboard. Their makeshift kitchens were no more than campfires with crusty black pots suspended over burning dried cow dung. Their children, black with soot and grime, wore little clothing. Their babies, quite naturally and practically, wore nothing below the waist. It was normal to see two-year-olds wandering alone among the beds and the rags. I wondered what kept them from walking into the busy traffic. Living on the streets they had no access to regular supplies of clean water or toilets, particularly in the centre of town. When I asked Dinesh about them, he used the word 'gitane', the French word for gypsy.

Driving through Jaipur was like being inside a kaleidoscope. At traffic lights, mothers sent babies, sometimes clothed but more often naked, tottering over to our car. Generous amounts of green snot were invariably spread over tiny smiling faces. They looked up at us and stretched out their little hands, fingers wiggling in the universal sign for alms. Huge billboards demanded our attention for the latest movie: mustachioed men with huge, round, leering, brown eyes, held curved swords in one hand and a bevy of dancing girls in the other. Fabric billowed out from hundreds of shops in great rainbows of

A Brush with India

designs and flashes of colour. The shoe stores displayed racks of uncomfortable-looking camel hide shoes. Touristy shops hung narrowly pleated cotton, ankle-length skirts high on shopfront windows where they fluttered in the wind like kites struggling to be free. Long lines of men holding all sorts of containers waited patiently for the milk brought in fresh each morning in large cream cans by men whose families have been dairy farmers for centuries. Smells of all sorts assaulted our noses, from the sweetest of oriental perfumes and incense to the pungent aroma of fresh cow dung, peanuts and chapatis frying in the morning sun. Two million people lived side by side with almost as many animals. Whole streets of screaming, chattering monkeys sat in tiny, pink palace windows waiting for their morning handout of food. Lofty camels looked down into our car and then ignored us with style. In the evening, an elephant painted with designs of birds and flowers trudged past us, heavy footed and tired like any other worker after a hard day.

Not far from Jaipur, only 11 kilometres (7 miles) through a small mountain pass, is Amber, the old capital of Jaipur. This fort and palace were built as a stronghold against invading armies. As we drove into the valley the first thing we saw were lines of elephants, their grey trunks swinging to the beat of their walk. Their mahouts appeared as tiny huddled men almost hidden behind the massive ears of their animals. Dinesh parked the car in the small town at the base of the fort and gave us our usual morning admonishments. The minute we were out of the car, souvenir sellers descended on us like a summer shower of rain. We were hassled and harassed. Would we like to buy puppets, hats (a good idea to bring one and a popular buy for those who did not), plastic elephants (not ivory, thank goodness) or postcards (crumpled edges held long in sweaty, hopeful hands)? We resisted the temptations and walked into the elephant compound. We had arrived at nine in the morning but we were still too late: 22 empty tourist buses stretched out along the road.

A set of stairs just high enough to reach the back of an elephant allowed us to turn around and plop ourselves down on 'our' animal. The road up to the fort was a steep climbing zigzag, only wide enough to let two elephants pass. Skirting

Jaipur and Bharatpur, Keoladeo National Park

under and around the tree-trunk legs of our pachyderm were the ever-present trinket pedlars. A favourite scheme was 'the misunderstanding'. When I handed down 6 rupees, a sum I had bargained long and hard for, hands would fly into the air, brows were wiped, eyes went round with incredibility. 'No, no, maharani' – suddenly I was a princess – 'it is 60 rupees.' I was left looking and feeling like a shrew denying food to starving orphans.

The ride up was jolting and jarring and I loved it. I was indulging in a fantasy, and this one cost little. Riding high on the back of an elephant approaching the high pavilions of Amber Fort was to glimpse history.

At the fort, and for a small fee, cups of tea and doughy English cakes waited for those who felt the need. But the elephants were more interesting. Our mahout, after a small tip, was happy to let me have a closer look at his elephant. It felt unnerving but exhilarating to be so close to such a large animal. He didn't seem to mind my curiosity. I laid myself against his trunk and reached up to feel his forehead with its prickly whiskers. I could feel his warmth, smell his wet straw-smelling breath. He had curious, tiny pale blue eyes and a total of 18 toes. Elephants have always been natural symbols of beauty and power for the maharajas and princes. In Mysore, not so long ago, 1000 elephants would be paraded through the city each year to celebrate the Hindu festival of Dassaorah. Each animal was draped in an elaborate blanket of interwoven flowers and their foreheads were studded with jewels and crowns of gold. Elephants are truly loved by the Indian people.

According to Hindu religion, the first elephants had wings. Since they had these wonderful attributes one of their favourite pastimes was to play among the clouds. One day, a tragic accident occurred. A group of these amazing elephants flew down to a beautiful tree and sat on its branches. Underneath the tree happened to be a priest sitting with his students. The branch broke, down went the elephants and several of the priest's students were killed. The priest, furious, called upon the gods to take the wings of the elephants away forever. Although the elephants could no longer fly, they continued to be friendly with their heavenly companions. It is because of this relationship that elephants have the divine ability to bring rain and abundant crops.

In the courtyard leading up to the palace, families of monkeys sat eyeing the easy touch, the 'phorens.' They studied the crowd long and closely. Suddenly, with their lips pulled back, and a fierce showing of teeth and a high-pitched scream, they would snatch a sticky bun from the hand of an unsuspecting, terrified tourist.

The palace sat like a crown on top of the hill, still redolent of its past splendour and victory, of violence and conquest. We were not allowed to take photos or video unless we paid for the privilege. Our cameras were taken away and put in lockers just in case we felt inclined to be 'cheaters'. The Rajputs liked beautiful, sumptuous surroundings. High in the maharaja's apartments was the hall of pleasure. In its main rooms, a water channel ran down through the middle, an early example of air conditioning. An elegant stairway led up to the hall of public audiences, where the maharaja would hear the requests of his subjects. Shaded, the room was filled with beautiful columns, each crowned with the carved head of an elephant. Latticework windows allowed even a small breeze to flow through and cool the sand-coloured courtyard. Steps leading off to the right went up to the Kali temple. Every day from the 16th century a small goat was sacrificed here. The Hindu goddess Kali is the wife of the powerful god Siva and her needs include blood and death-sacrifice. In the days when sacrifice was a daily occurrence, the small statue situated here would have been decorated with marigold flowers, holy images, candy and small pieces of jewellery, or candles – anything one could afford. The black-faced Kali has a large lolling tongue dripping with blood and four arms. She wears snakes in her hair and a necklace of the skulls of her sons. Appeasement of Kali means that occasionally she allows a barren woman to conceive. Bleating terrified animals were brought to the altar and swiftly decapitated as the frenzied voices of the priests cried out, 'Kali, Kali, Kali.' Hysterical women, waiting in hope and desperation for a child, would rush forward, throw themselves to the floor and drench their shawls in blood. Holding them to their bosoms, they would pray for the miracle of conception.

Jaipur and Bharatpur, Keoladeo National Park

In 1980, government law finally stopped the sacrifice of animals at Amber. I wonder what poverty-stricken women do now to ease the pain of infertility. A barren woman in India, especially if she is poor, often leads a miserable life. Even her parents may feel ashamed and shun her. What else has she to give to her husband's demanding family? A barren first wife will lead to second and third wives who will give what she cannot. The sacrifice of a goat seems trivial for hope and a miracle.

Jaipur was an extraordinary place to go shopping. The grandeur of the rich brocades and silks to be bought in India has enchanted women and couturiers for centuries. Italian designers like Ungaro and Valentino have turned increasingly to the skill of Indian craftsmen. The Kashmiri shawl is so fine and so famous; as everyone knows, it can be drawn through the circumference of a ring. An eye-catching place at the Ganapati Plaza, Rana's Silks and Sarees, was our first attempt at shopping. We were totally unprepared. Gaston wanted to buy me a sari. It seemed a simple wish. All we needed to do was to walk into the store and pick out a piece of cloth. An armed guard at the double glass and brass doors directed us inside. (I was immediately reminded of the first and only time I went into Chanel's in Paris. It seemed every eye was upon me, I felt horridly unsure of what I should do next. Should I bluff it out and flounce around, looking and nodding, frowning and acting as if I could only be tempted with something better? Or should I slink out, knowing damn well that I couldn't afford anything and would have nowhere to wear it anyway?) This time it definitely was going to be the bluff. Two men took us up a winding staircase reminiscent of Gone With the Wind and settled us into plush chairs. 'Would we like tea?' No, I thought, I'd like to get out of here. I smiled sweetly, let my wrists relax over the end of the armchair, and replied, 'Thank you so very much.'

In front of us was a low catwalk about a metre wide and behind it were six men, who hovered over garments hanging in glass and brass wardrobes. I had never seen such colours in cloth, from the brightest to the softest hue and not one of them garish. I immediately fell in love with a creation in a clear buttercup yellow silk with a satin finish. It had three pieces: a short-sleeved top, a floor-length skirt and a matching whisper-thin shawl. Hand-embroidered all over with pearls and sequins, it was exquisitely finished and impressive. When I recovered, I realised, to my alarm, that Gaston meant to buy it. I asked the price. Gauche move. 'Madam, I am sure the price is of no consequence, if your husband wishes to bestow upon his wife such a fine garment.' My worthy husband's move: 'How much is it?'

To be fair, it was a bargain: US$500 was only the equivalent of a few weeks' groceries, or the price of a man's suit. Did I toss good common sense to the winds and let Gaston buy it just because of a romantic whim? And for what occasion would I wear it?

I manoeuvred a compromise. We chose another at US$180, which was just as beautiful but had a handful fewer pearls. It is true that, after several breathless sessions of showing it off to my family and friends, it now sits in my closet. But I keep the door open enough so that I get a glimpse of it now and then.

We didn't realise we had gone to the most expensive shop in Jaipur. Saris can be bought for as little as $3. There are a few things to be aware of. For instance, Indian women are much shorter than Americans or New Zealanders. A Western person will need a longer sari, because it will allow more pleats at the front and a longer drop over the shoulder. In Varanasi, the source of the *crème de la crème* of silk, the length tends to be 5 metres, 6 if possible. Also, the fabric should not be one that wrinkles easily. Sometimes you can get a pamphlet that explains how to wrap the sari in the right way. I went into a sari shop in an expensive hotel, pretended I was staying there, and asked for one. The best way is to have someone show you. It takes a few practice runs but the secret is in the safety pins. It is also necessary to have a long cotton draw-cord skirt and a short-sleeved bare midriff blouse, which are worn as undergarments. The skirt is essential because the sari is held up by it.

I had never seen such a collection of glittering temptation as Indian jewellery. When I returned home, I went to our local jeweller and asked him if there was some way of learning how to determine the value and authenticity of precious gems. He denied such a thing was available to the public. But then he would, wouldn't he? The type and price of items were endless. The problem was knowing whether you were getting value for money and what you were allowed to bring back into New Zealand. There were high – and low-priced jewellery shops just as there were with clothing.

By accident I went to an élite jewellery store while waiting for Dinesh to collect some gasoline money. It was impressive, with plush thick carpets and the obligatory glass and brass. Emeralds, rubies, diamonds, earrings, bracelets, rings cried out in endless rows of enticement; wisely Gaston refused to be coaxed from the plush armchair.

Later that night I went on a shopping spree with Gopal Singh, the tuk-tuk driver who waited patiently in front of our hotel. He said he was the one man who knew where to find everything and at the 'best price'. We set off into the dark, three-wheeling around corners and finally arriving at a warehouse stacked from floor to ceiling with tablecloths, sheets, bedcovers, cushion covers and bedspreads. There were rows and rows of shelves 6 metres high. More merchandise took up almost every available spot of floor space. All I could do was request the item, size and the colour I had in mind. There was no question of rummaging. 'Could you please leave me alone for 12 hours while I have a look at the 30,000 – who knows maybe 50,000 — tablecloths?' I went next door to the clothing room, passing hundreds of white linen parcels waiting to be shipped overseas. I was embarrassed, staggered by the sheer quantity. It was impossible to select anything amid such hills, mountains and very few valleys of clothes. I bought three tablecloths and we were off again into the night. The next stop was a manufacturing jeweller, a large factory with people working in every room. I was shown into a showroom with an obvious lack of glass and brass and no plush armchairs. It wasn't easy to decide but I finally bought five silver and garnet bracelets and 10 delightful toe rings.

Dinesh was highly disappointed with me. This time, apparently I had overstepped my right to be his friend. He had told me not, certainly not, to go with any tuk-tuk driver to buy anything – nought, zero and zilch. 'Great cheaters.' Gopal had spent the morning telling him how much commission he received.

A Brush with India

Drivers make commissions from taking their clients to factories and showrooms; they sometimes make as much as 50 per cent. If possible and you have the time it is much better to visit these places on your own. Since I paid a total of $18 for the three tablecloths and $175 for the jewellery, I wondered how big a sum this could be? I would have had to pay three or four times that amount for the same items back home, even if I could find them. In retrospect I probably could have saved money if I had waited for Dinesh. I fell for the sad eyes and persistence of the tuk-tuk driver. I was suitably penitent and promised I would ask Dinesh first if I was ever tempted again.

Dinesh told me he had been 'a very, very lucky man'. He felt that the constant Moslem/Hindu conflict posed a very real threat to his life. According to the newspaper, there had been an armed clash between 'two groups of people' at the holy shrine of Sufi saint, Khwaja Moinnuddin Cristi in Ajmer. Twenty-five people were injured and two killed the day we left. There was now a curfew. I understood Dinesh's recent moodiness.

There was more. He was running out of money and we were only halfway through our trip. He was angry and feeling vulnerable and hoped he could locate the people who should be paying him. We wanted to leave the next day: Gaston was still not well enough to paint and had now set his sights on Agra. We remembered we had the telephone number to call if there was a problem with the car or the driver. Cautiously we decided to leave this to Dinesh to deal with. We didn't want to risk hurting his pride, again.

In Jodhpur, it was possible to buy a book entitled *A Princess Remembers* written by Gayatra Devi, the daughter of a maharaja and the widow of the famous and last maharaja of Jaipur. Her life was one of international journeys, surrounded by hundreds of servants. She had known only the highest standards of luxury all of her life. She talked of her husband, Jai, the 'dashing polo-player', and the intense love she still had for him, since his tragic death at the age of 59. She was Jai's third wife and lived with his other two wives in seemingly great love and understanding.

As a woman, I wondered if I could share my husband with

several other wives. She made it sound a loving and normal thing to do. And how could a person live in so much luxury in the middle of so much misery, with so many deprived, even starving people around her? The most interesting part of her book was the description of how the maharajas existed before 1970, how they held the people together and how the population looked to them to settle their problems. In Rajasthan, and particularly the capital of Jaipur, this was certainly true. Jai was there to listen, to find and give food in times of drought or monsoon, to reassure. He was both a human father figure, and a visible god, who cared when required. This was the system that held the Indian states together. The people existed together: the supremely wealthy and the desperately poor, the upper caste all the way down to the untouchables. In its way, it worked because people had a job, had a purpose in life. Your caste meant your work, whether rajah or shoemaker, musician or mortician. Even today, with a literacy rate of only 38 per cent, most people in Rajasthan have work, be it ever so humble. It is not enough but at least people do not suffer the horrible malaise and distortion of uselessness.

Just before Independence in 1947 there were 565 maharajas, nawabs, rajahs and rulers who reigned as hereditary sovereigns over one-third of India. One of them was the richest man in the world. At the opposite end was a man who had a kingdom smaller than 50 square kilometres. A few gave their unique fraternity a bad name by indulging in excesses, but many offered their subjects a much better life and economy than the British. With their dazzling jewels and palaces, their tigers and herds of elephants, they were an extraordinary group. Each had, on average, five wives, 12 children, nine elephants, three Roll-Royces and two railway cars. They were, in 1947, on the edge of extinction.

The palace museum at Jaipur was a great disappointment, only a remnant, the bones without the flesh, although it was only 25 years since the buildings had been dismantled. The blend of Mogul and Rajasthani architecture was still visible, and there were impressive collections of royal costumes and weaponry, wonderful examples of their time.

In the morning, with many apologies from Dinesh, we made

a stop to pick up the rest of money he needed for our final 12 days with the car. The travel agency's attitude toward Dinesh was wrong. He took the responsibility for the long, difficult and dangerous drive. They could have, at the very least, made sure he slept and ate well, and didn't have to worry about running out of money.

We left Jaipur via Amber and joined the main highway at 10 in the morning. Five minutes later we ran straight into a traffic jam. Just east of Jaipur, on the major Delhi to Agra road, was a village that repaired trucks. It runs parallel to the road with garages on both sides and took one hour just to drive through. As if they were soldiers and this was an annual check-up, great armies of vehicles came to this place for repairs. As far as the eye could see, they lay in various stages, many undergoing surgery, many having parts replaced, many more just waiting in line for a mechanic. Men in all states of anxiety were watching over their vehicles. Car mechanics rushed around with oil sticks in their hands. Amputations littered the road. Many trucks lay ominously quiet, covered with a sheet of dust. We threaded our little Ambassador car in and out of the platoons of transport. We were like a weevil in a field of cotton, unable to see our way, except for small patches of asphalt. It was frustratingly slow. It was fascinating. It was live cinema.

Although it was only 250 kilometres/150 miles from Jaipur, it was seven hours before we arrived at Bharatpur. We were told we must not miss the famous bird sanctuary, Keoladeo Ghana National Park. Although some people get a great kick out of bird watching, it was not something we had considered before and our enthusiasm was not exactly wild. Keoladeo Park had a lot of accommodation at all price levels. We found a hotel that seemed better than most and, after a little haggling, it was nearly the same price as those less attractive. The room, large, not overly clean but adequate, was on the second floor of a two-storey building with a wide verandah overlooking a garden filled with old-fashioned hollyhocks. The man who helped with our luggage, quite hospitably enquired if, after our long journey, we would like a cup of tea. This was delivered along with an apology: there was going to be a special function in the dining room so would we mind having an early dinner?

We ordered from the menu delivered to our room and the food turned out to be excellent. The Hotel Eagles Nest knew how to cater for tourists. All was well, apart from a few mosquitoes and a shower fitted with a monsoon head, impossible to direct or turn off. Our bathroom quickly turned into a swamp.

The menu, so politely delivered to our room, had one thing missing: the prices. When we paid our bill the following morning, the cost of the dinner, which included the tea and an extra bottle of water, came to double the price of the room, triple the amount of any meal we had before. Dinesh was there when we paid the bill, and he had only one word to describe the situation. I tossed the bottle of water in the back of the car and we set off down the road to go bird watching at Keoladeo Park.

There was a tiny entry fee and then it was possible to walk around the park or even bicycle (some hotels had them for rent), but the usual way to get around was by cycle-rickshaw. Dinesh had another 'brother' who just happened to be a cycle-rickshaw driver, who pedalled us around the park.

Wondering what we were doing there and why, we set off down the sealed track, which crosses through the middle of the park's 29 kilometres. The seats of the rickshaw were impossibly thin and we kept shifting our bottoms trying to alleviate the sore spots. It was a foggy morning. There seemed little to see. Bushes hugged the sides of the road, rickshaws passed in the other direction. We waved at drivers and tourists going the other way. Our driver chatted enthusiastically, trying his best to get us interested in the murky surroundings. It was like being agnostics at a church service.

Before long, the mist began to thin and the sun started to filter through the clouds. Monkeys, used to the presence of tourists, scampered over the road. Furry, cupped hands reached up and begged for food. The driver kept chattering on: 'We will find very big python'. Python? This slightly built cheerful man, who weighed a quarter of our combined weights, finally succeeded in talking his way into our thoughts and our curiosity; for 70 cents an hour he shared with us his extensive knowledge of Keoladeo Park and as we started to listen to this Minister of the Wild we found a revelation we had not expected.

A Brush with India

The creation of the park was an accident. In the late 1890s, the Maharaja of Bharatpur, inspired by a visit to Britain, decided to create his own game reserve. To do so, he deepened and extended a large area of marshland, constructed dykes and tracks and directed water supplies. Enormous numbers of birds were slaughtered over the following years. Stone plaques stand in the middle of the park recording the shoots for the first half of this century. They are rather quaintly headed, 'on the occasion of the visit of' and then list the dates and the amounts of 'bags' taken.

1902 December	H.E. Lord Kitchener and Lord Curzon 520 birds with 17 guns
1916 November	H.E. Viceroy Lord Chelmsford 4260 birds with 50 guns
1936 November	H.E. the Viceroy Lord Linlithgow 4273 birds with 39 guns

What did they do with 4000 birds? They might have given them to the surrounding farmers, who have been in a state of despondency ever since the bird reserve began. The marsh birds, particularly the wild geese, eat their crops.

Shoots were still taking place in the 1960s but by that time a conservation society had started to manage the area as a sanctuary. It was declared a national park in 1981 and made a world heritage park in 1984. There are known to be 1200 species of birds in India: over 400 species make Keoladeo their permanent nesting site.

We began to feel that we were in a place that might be interesting after all. This was an entirely new macrocosm. Our rickshaw wallah was very knowledgeable about bird habits and identification. He carried a set of binoculars and for a 'small added price' we could borrow them. He started by pointing out the huge nests of the painted stork, so named because they look as though some mad artist has thrown a pot of red and orange over their white plumage.

It felt luxurious to ride in an open vehicle underneath the boughs of huge trees. The sun warmed the air and where before we might not have noticed anything special, our guide quietly pointed out some new feathered marvel. Aside from his whispers, the only sounds came from the birds, such as the brilliant green parrots, which made shrieking screeches when we came near their nests. Another bird that caught our attention was the red wattled lapwing, which had the irritating quality of signalling a warning when we tried to approach it: 'Did-he-do-it, did-he-do-it?'

Little purple moorhens trotted around in shallows, fussing with the leaves of aquatic plants. They reminded me of the pukeko, a native bird common in New Zealand. The male, we learned, has an interesting courtship display. He gives his 'intended' gifts of waterweeds, usually accompanying the offering with elaborate bows and noisy chuckles. By the river we saw a familiar bird, which gave itself away by its iridescent blue flash – a kingfisher.

Because it was the end of winter, there was lush growth everywhere. With plenty of marshes and lakes, ecosystems and swamps, trees and grassland, this was a perfect sanctuary for the world's diminishing bird population. February was a good time to come to Bharatpur: migrant birds were making their way to the park from thousands of kilometres away. We saw fat brown graylag geese with orange beaks, swimming in circles. Incapable of silence, they honked away at each other, having a great gossip session. Some birds come from as far away as Iceland, others from Russia. We heard about the shy Tibetan bar-headed goose, named for the black stripes on its snow-white head. There had been a steep decline in its numbers over recent years because of changing conditions in Tibet. The people of Tibet, being Buddhist, regarded all forms of life as sacred and could never kill or harm a living creature, so these geese were extremely tame, gentle and unafraid of man. But when the Chinese invaded all animals were regarded as a source of food.

Siberian cranes are now listed as critically endangered. With their red and pinkish faces, snow-white plumage, sleek bodies, black wings and long tails they are unusual and elegant. Three birds came to the sanctuary in 1960 and over the following five years their number increased to over 200. But then their numbers started to decline. By 1994 and 1995 not one Siberian crane came to the park but in 1996, on the first day of winter, four birds flew into the park. It was a rickshaw wallah like ours who made the first sighting. The falling number of Siberian cranes seems to be a result of the continuing warfare in Afghanistan. As birds migrate over airways known to them for centuries, they are shot down for meat.

The Saurus crane, however, can be seen in healthy abundance. In India no one would wilfully harm this bird: to do so would bring bad luck. The peacock is the national bird of India but this crane would be no less likely a choice. Sometimes it becomes so tame that it is kept as a pet. The Mogul emperor, Jehangir, an astute naturalist and sportsman, held these birds in high regard and made exhaustive notes on them. He wrote extensively about their most endearing quality: they mate for life. Never far apart from one another, they even fly together. It is said that when one bird dies, the second bird dies soon after.

Flocks of common ducks arrive at the park in winter and 80 different types have now been found within the sanctuary. There has been considerable banding over recent years and recoveries of these birds have been found as far away as 5000 kilometres (3000 miles).

Little yellow egrets strutted past us like Daffy Duck look-a-likes. In the watery haze we could see man-made islands planted with acacia trees, the ground underneath already yellow with fallen blossom. In the far distance we could see a blackbuck through binoculars.

The pythons had a cosy little number in front of a temple. We always tended to forget that, in India, all life, is sacred. To a Hindu, something as repulsive as a python could be an incarnated relative. The pythons burrow in deep holes near the entrance of the temple and come out to bathe in the sun and eat rats that wander around in search of titbits. How did that work in the Hindu scheme of reincarnation? I'm sure there's a suitable answer – probably many.

Chapter 7
Fatehpur Sikri

WE LEFT THE BIRD sanctuary two hours later, feeling as if we had discovered a new world. The wild beauty, the knowledge so generously given with such good humour and the luxury of riding through the woodlands in the early morning sun – all were unexpected pleasures.

We returned to the car and took off down the road towards Agra 56 kilometres (33 miles) away. In the back seat I was puzzled to notice water on the floor. I knew the bottle of water I had placed there still had its sealed cap and the plastic cellophane wrap on the top was intact. I moved the bottle to the other side of the car but after a few kilometres another patch of water appeared there. After a few seconds of examination, I discovered a small half-moon incision along the edge of the cap, neatly cut and big enough to allow a bottle to be refilled. When the bottle was standing upright there was no danger of water leaking but lying on the floor of the car it soon began to drip. This was the second time I'd been tricked with bottled water.

Dinesh had a surprise for us: Fatehpur Sikri. We thought we were finally on our way to Agra. Why would we want to stop now? Gaston was less than impressed: he was feeling better and anxious to get on with his work. Reluctantly we handed over an impossibly small sum to the gatekeepers who allowed traffic to continue up the hill. We hoped this wasn't going to take long. We drove up a short distance, then Dinesh parked the car and nodded us towards some sandstone steps.

Some places in the world bring out special feelings in people: an impression of excitement, anticipation, like having front row seats for a long awaited night at the theatre or opera. These places are very often known tourists' haunts such as Yosemite National Park in California, the city of Paris, the mountain village of Delphi in Greece – and Fatehpur Sikri in India. Do we feel this way because such places seem familiar because we have seen them so often in films or photographs? Or does the feeling spring from something mysterious, special and inviting about the places themselves?

Fatehpur Sikri, built by Akbar, the greatest of all the Mogul emperors, is a ghost city, completely intact. It feels new and ready to move into. We would not have been at all surprised if the moving vans were just waiting for the tourists to leave so they could start shifting in the furniture, the rugs and the canary cages. To get in sufficient food for the animals in Akbar's time they would also have needed enough hay and water for 1000 elephants, 30,000 horses and 1400 tame deer, not to mention untold numbers of camels.

With one phantom arm around my shoulder, Akbar showed me the sights. He led me from room to room, courtyard to courtyard. I was running everywhere afraid I might miss something. 'What's this? What's that?' I kept saying. His royal self kept turning me in different directions, asking, 'Is it like anything you have seen before?' Here is where my musicians sat, looking as if they were floating on a pond of water. Have you seen these carvings? Look over there. Isn't it all wonderful, extraordinary?' I was so utterly impressed. I was so damned ignorant. Who the hell was Akbar?

To understand his story, his ancestors and his descendants, is to understand a large part of the story of India. The Moslem conquest of India is one of the bloodiest in history. The religions of the Hindus, the Jains and those belonging to Buddha are all religions that hold the philosophy of pacifism and reverence for life uppermost in their beliefs. The Hindus had plenty of courage but little taste for blood. If they had feuds, they were small internal squabbles; because of their relaxed ways they failed to think beyond their own borders. They had armies, but were not capable of dealing with the sophistication of the Moslems. They were almost defenceless and easily outmanoeuvred by the superior Islamic armies. Clumsy elephants and hand-held maces were no match against battalions of trained horse-mounted troops, skilled in feint and retreat.

Even before the first major attacks by the Moslems, India had always been subject to invaders: Huns, Afghans, Persians and Greeks all considered it a smash-and-grab opportunity. This is one of the most important things to understand about the

Fatehpur Sikri

inhabitants of the Indian continent: they have been oppressed for thousands of years. The English, the last raiders, left them better off, but financially crippled, divided and vulnerable. To understand the intense need to be a self-governing and strongly unified nation is to comprehend the euphoric frenzy and jubilance at their first testing of an atomic bomb. This is their big stick, their powerful warning to would-be invaders. Turning the other cheek is reluctantly but firmly over. Hindu India intends to look after itself.

In AD 632, immediately after the death of Mohammed, the one true prophet of Allah, his disciples spread in all directions to convert the infidels. Looking at a map of the Middle East, it is easy to see the logical progression from Arabia. They spread north, then east and west, through what we now call Iran, Afghanistan, Baluchistan and, importantly, Pakistan. By the eighth century, this first contingent went as far as the great Thar Desert in Rajasthan. There the Rajput warriors stopped them and their conquest was halted for the next 300 years.

In AD 1001 Mahmud Ghazni changed the course of history in India forever. This Turkish chieftain from Afghanistan, this outstanding warrior, clearly knew what he wanted from life: power and wealth. Within the pretext of religion, over 20 years he made 17 raids into India through the Northwest Passage, often slaughtering up to 100,000 inhabitants at a time. In his eyes, if the people were not Moslem, they were pagans and should be exterminated. He took so many people as slaves; that they became a worthless commodity. As a religious zealot he, quite naturally, took great pleasure and pride in destroying non-Moslem temples that had been standing for centuries. After having expressed the greatest admiration for the architecture of one Hindu shrine, and recognising that its construction would have taken 200 years of manual labour, he burnt it to the ground. He astonished other warrior-lords with his vast quantities of silver and gold and, 'jewels and pearls and rubies shining like sparks, like wine congealed with ice, and emeralds like fresh sprigs of myrtle, and diamonds in size and weight like pomegranates'. By the end of his campaign he was one of the richest and most honoured Islamic potentates in history. He killed millions but it was only the beginning of blood letting in the name of Allah. By

A Brush with India

passing on his knowledge of the Northwest Passage he made it an open doorway for all others. Reigning for a third of a century, he knelt at every encounter, and asked the blessing of God. Moslem historians rank him as one of the greatest monarchs of his time; for Hindus the very name of Mahmud Ghazni is the embodiment of brutality.

The two religions, Hindu and Moslem, are so opposed in doctrine that it would be hard to find more differing beliefs. Hindus believe in many gods and many prophets. Moslems believe in one god and one prophet, Mohammed. Hindus hold the cow as sacred, regard it as a mother figure and revere it. Moslems eat cows. The Hindu religions thrive on idolatry, in the form of statues and likenesses, in temples and also in houses, vehicles and businesses. The Moslems believe idolatry to be blasphemy, and any representation of God is deeply against their ideals. Hindus believe strongly that all men are not equal. Brahmans, the Hindu priests and upper caste, are near gods and everyone beneath them has a descending order and merit. Moslems believe that all men are created equal. (Only men not women: women are inferior.) Hindus believe in many lives and in repeated reincarnations. Moslems say you only have one life and then it is heaven or hell. The Hindu faith does not try to convert people. In fact, you cannot be converted: you have to be born a Hindu. Moslems thought it normal to kill people if they didn't convert. The Hindu religion is mostly peaceful, open-minded, accepting and not meddlesome. Some Moslems can be fanatically religious extremists.

Thinking about the colossal wealth gained by Mahmud, future Moslem invaders could not resist the temptation of further treachery. It was profitable, easy and honourable because they saw it as an act of God. By 1186 Delhi had been captured, its temples and monuments reduced to rubble, its inhabitants demoralised and crushed. Islam historians tell of the first sultan, Kutb-d Din Aibak, the 'Slave Sultan', who was born a slave and rose to his position by sheer grit, brutality and cunning. Balan, another sultan punished rebel Hindus by letting elephants dance up and down on their bodies. Humans were skinned, stuffed with straw and hung on gates to cities to remind the infidel of Moslem power.

It was a common practice for Moslem sons to kill fathers, especially ruling fathers who lingered for too long. Sultan Mohammad bin Tughlak started his career this way and not only became a scholar in letters, mathematics, philosophy and physics, but surpassed his predecessors in unabated horror. He had so many people put to death that his executioners could not keep up with the disposal of the dead.

The Moslem Sultans thought nothing of killing, raping and total annihilation. Every malicious, bloodthirsty rite was acted out. Little in European history comes close to their barbaric practices, yet these rulers were amazing tacticians and impeccable war analysts, gifted with consummate courage. They believed they had God on their side, and they would conquer the world. Their plan was to reduce the Hindu people to such a level of poverty that they could not fight or think of an insurrection. The secret and sorrow of the political history of India has always been in the weakness of its religious divisions and its abject poverty. In the days of the sultans, heavy taxes so burdened the Hindus that the only things that remained unalterable, were the heat of the day and their belief in their gods.

The first conqueror of the sultans of Delhi was a Turkish warrior who wisely adopted the Moslem religion as a defence and then set off to conquer the Indian city. It didn't matter that the inhabitants were already Moslems: perhaps they weren't true believers. Anyway, he wanted it. Equipped with a royal lineage and fearless courage, he proceeded. Tamerlane took everything, but he took it all back home to Samarkand, leaving behind only death, famine, ruin and chaos. Delhi was later taken over by yet another Moslem sultanate. Taxes were reinforced for another century. Cruelty and repression continued.

But the worst invaders and most devastating were yet to come. In the 13th century, from the frozen steppes of Asia, the Mongols appeared. Mongols were the savage followers of Genghis Khan; the Moguls were a more settled, civilised people, partly of Turkish origin, who had generally accepted Allah as their god and become Moslems. Confusingly, the Hindus, even today, call all northern Moslems Moguls. The vital difference between the Moslem and the Mongol invaders was that the former brought with them the finest and the most sophisticated culture the world had to offer. They also offered the refinements of ancient Persia and classical Greece. The Mongols, on the other hand, had a culture based on senseless cruelty and mindless destruction. It existed on a diet of killing, burning and destruction. They lived like animals, thirsting for the next kill, the next molestation. They didn't have religion as an excuse, as the Moslems did. They plundered the world from Japan right through to Europe. Genghis Khan and his hordes killed every scholar, burned every library and deliberately destroyed everything in their path. They managed to take the normal evolution of knowledge by the throat and almost strangle it to death.

The third conquest of India came in the early 1500s. In other parts of the world at the same time, the Inca civilisation fell to its death, butchered by the blade of Spain, cruelly administered by Pizarro in the name of Christianity. In England, Henry the Eighth sent a message to the Pope of Rome that his services would no longer be needed.

Descended from both Tamerlane and Genghis Khan, a new ruler was about to make his entrance into the Indian continent. At 12 years of age, Babur became the overlord of his small kingdom, Farghana. According to historians, he inherited the strength and strategic ability of his predecessors, their wisdom and their religion but, incomprehensibly, not their brutality. Three years later, at 15 he was nearly captured near Samarkand. At 22, outnumbered by 10 to 1, he went on to take Delhi and Agra. (One spoil of war was the immense Koh-I-Noor diamond, now part of the English crown jewels.) Babur, affectionately known as the Lion, stayed in his new country although, as with so many immigrants before and after him, it never really felt like home. In his new kingdom he settled down and wrote poetry. He created Persian style gardens to remind him of his birthplace. He gathered flowers from Kabul and named 34 varieties of tulips. Babur established the greatest and most magnanimous kingdom of any of the foreign infiltrators. Finally, after centuries of horrendous abuse, northern India began to settle down to a modicum of peace.

Babur, who was the grandfather of Akbar, died in a surprising way. Legend says he made a deal with God. His son, Humayun, had taken ill and Babur offered his life in exchange for Humayun's. God, in His mysterious way, took him seriously. No sooner did Babur begin to take ill than Humayun began to improve. If God had Humayun's CV, He certainly had hidden motives because the child had a serious opium habit and was, like many sons of great men, inept and unable to make decisions. Humayun was a mother's boy, too.

It wasn't long before he lost his father's kingdom and it took 15 long years to get even a little part of it back. In the fourth year of his exile Humayun fell headlong in love – so much so, that he became an embarrassment to everyone with his constant grovelling pleas for marriage. The daughter of a Persian had taken his heart. Finally, the two were married and he got his kingdom back. His first son, Abu-ul-fath Jalal-ud-din Muhammad Akbar, the greatest of all the Mogul kings, was born on 15 October 1542, in a humble tent where his parents had taken refuge in the desert. It is said Humayun leaped with joy when he saw his little son's horoscope.

It wasn't until 1554 that Humayun succeeded in retrieving some of his lost fortunes, and then only with the help of friendly Persian forces. Lahore and Delhi were regained but valuable land in the Punjab and south of Delhi was lost. Six months after re-entering Delhi he slipped down a flight of stairs and died. Akbar, who was then 13 years old, became the heir to the Mogul dynasty.

Understanding the history of the previous events of India makes the appearance of a man like Akbar seems astonishing. Although he had the best of teachers, he was totally illiterate. He became one of the greatest humanitarians of his time, but remained unable to read or write for the rest of his life.

Bairam Khan, Akbar's faithful general, not only looked after the empire belonging to a child, but also consolidated it. When Akbar took command at 18, his kingdom was secure. It stretched as far west as Afghanistan, Baluchistan and Pakistan, and east to the Bay of Bengal. Kashmir was also taken.

Akbar was a supreme athlete. He excelled at all sports, was a keen polo player and a perfect equestrian. One of his specialities was jumping on the back of half-wild male elephants and subduing them into capitulation. He was

A Brush with India

shrewd, intelligent and ambitious and had a great love for danger. Even at an early age he showed great force and command. When invited to assume the title of Gazni, Killer of Infidels, he did not hesitate: stepping up to a Hindu official, he chopped the man's head off with one swift blow. A short time later he took off for Gujarat where an uprising had taken place, marching at the side of 3000 horsemen over a distance of 1000 kilometres (600 miles). He arrived nine days later and by the end of the following two days the revolt was over. He rushed into battle, not as a follower of his capable armies but as a leader. Akbar's honour as a brilliant and fearless warrior was assured.

His next achievement, something never achieved by foreign invaders, proved what a gifted tactician he was. The Rajputs chiefs of Rajasthan, the outstanding warriors of the Thar Desert, had never been brought completely under control by the Moslems or Mongolians and had retained their kingdoms. Despite suffering some defeats, they retained their authority and remained a threat to whoever became a conqueror in India. Akbar did the impossible. Two hundred yoked teams of oxen, struggling, straining up the impossible narrow ravines of a Rajput hilltop fortress, forced their way to the top. Drummers sitting astride cannon sounded a steady beat, encouraging men and animals to pull to the end of their endurance. With guns, knives and whips and suffering impossible heat, overwhelming the Rajputs was their only objective. When the fort was on the verge of capitulation Akbar went inside, not to kill but to put forward a proposition: as the fort was soon to be taken, would it not be better to surrender without further bloodshed? He had the foresight to offer the one thing that others had overlooked: he promised to reward these rulers not only with the continuation of their offices but also with his acceptance of them as leaders. Consequently, the rulers of Rajasthan became allies instead of enemies. Akbar had understood the etiquette, the idea of gallantry so vital to the Rajput psyche.

Then, astonishingly, he took a Rajput princess from Amber and made her his queen. She was, of course, Hindu. How unthinkable for the rulers who had come before him. At this union, the establishment of a Hindu-Moslem bloodline became validated for eternity. Purist Moslems must have hated him for it. Not only did he take Hindu wives but he also appointed Hindu generals. By this alliance, military stabilisation in the Mogul Empire was assured. For the first time, a multinational and multireligious society began to take form. What is so different about Akbar was not only his compassion and understanding, but also his strength to change all lives for the better.

In the painful area of taxes he made huge changes. He sent assessors to study each individual area, so that he might better understand the yield of different types of land. This determined the fairest tax possible. The most daring change was the abolishment of the Jizya, the hated head tax against the non-Moslems. All destruction of Hindu temples ceased. Child marriages were forbidden, and also suttee: widows were encouraged to remarry. Akbar abolished the slavery of captives. Animals were no longer permitted to be sacrificed. In all things he weighed fairness according to his own sense of justice. If orthodox customs dictated rules, he ignored them and used his own judgement. He didn't just listen to his advisers. Akbar was a man of action and total involvement in everything he did. Disguised in the clothing of his poorest people, at night he went into the cities to see and hear for himself about the conditions of his subjects.

In the arts, which Akbar extolled, he embraced the advancement of letters, poetry, music and art. He would sit and listen for hours to the fine cadences of well-written poetry: he loved one poet so much that he made him a general. He encouraged the mixture of Moslem, Persian, Turkish and Hindu arts and customs. He set up private studios where artists could work without worrying about where their next chapati was coming from. Each week there was a grand showing of work. The best artists were rewarded not only with honour but with money – lots of it.

Akbar's favourite subject was religion. Every Friday he would summon religious leaders to an afternoon of religious discussion. Reading the recorded journal of his life it is easy to see Akbar was a serious philosopher of religion. No religion was barred from his interest and his intensive study. He invited crowds of Brahmans, Jains, Zoroastrians, Moslems, Jews and

A Brush with India

Christians to explain their beliefs in depth. He abandoned his Moslem faith and for a time took to wearing Hindu religious marks on his forehead. Akbar ordered the entire New Testament, brought by the Portuguese missionaries, meticulously translated into Persian. Then he had every page read to him. As evidence of his own neutrality and a pledge of peace he took additional wives of the Brahmin, Buddhist and Moslem faiths. Nevertheless, the religious divisions of his kingdom worried him. His final decision was to form a new religion, Sulh-I-Kul, where he was head of the church. These were not the dreams of an omnipotent dictator, but a sincere effort to bring the ideals of all his people together. He explained, 'We ought, therefore, to bring them all into one, but in such fashion that they should be both "one" and "all"; with the great advantage of not losing what is good in any one religion, while gaining whatever is better in another. In that way honour would be rendered to God, peace would be given to the people, and security to the empire.'

He had the best intentions but the concept was doomed from the start. What was great for some seemed seditious to others. Cows were not to be slaughtered: the Hindus were happy; the Moslems were not. Vegetarianism was compulsory for 100 days of the year. Garlic and onions were also prohibited. The Hindu won again. The fast of Ramadan, the pilgrimage to Mecca and the building of mosques were all prohibited. It could not possibly work in such ingrained tradition. Few bothered trying. Yet it did weaken religious and racial fanaticism and, in a modest way, it did achieve some racial unity.

Understanding the kind of man Akbar was makes it easier to perceive the mystique of Fatehpur Sikri. There are so many outstanding sites in India that it is impossible to say one is better than another, yet Fatehpur has a magnetism that is immediate – perhaps because it is a ghost city, empty for the last 400 years. For 150,000 nights the moon has risen on empty red sandstone streets. Nothing but the cry of a bird, the trickle of rainwater, has broken its long silent nights. It remains sharply well defined, elusive and haunting. Built on top of a high rocky spur, with the plain below stretching in every direction, it sits on its own dusty red cloud. The

Fatehpur Sikri

personality of its owner rushes forward to every visitor.

It was with great joy and love that Akbar began building the new city of Fatehpur Sikri. He felt it was a lucky place, for a holy man had once told him three sons would be born to him on this site. When his queen, who had previously only given birth to stillborn babies, became pregnant again he began his new city. In 1572, when Akbar was 30 years old, Jahangir, his little prince, was placed alive and healthy in his father's arms.

The years that followed must have been the happiest of Akbar's life. He was not a handsome man: he had long arms and legs, narrow eyes that were a remnant of his Mongolian ancestors and a wart on the end of his nose. Still, tellingly, his biographers say his shining eyes sparkled, 'like the sea in sunshine'. He had a visible serenity and dignity. He was always neatly and simply dressed with a small brocaded cap, plain blouse and trousers, a few jewels and went barefoot. His bodyguards were Tartar women who carried small daggers in their clothing.

As to his character, he entered everything with exuberance. For six years after Jahangir was born, he concentrated on building Fatehpur Sikri. He was so devoted to his task that sometimes he quarried the large pieces of stone along with the workers. He was seen to practise carving ornate reliefs, though only master craftsmen, men who had been trained since childhood, from father to son, could create the wonderful carvings of his sandstone city.

One of the most striking buildings is the Diwan-I-Khas, a two-storey, red sandstone square topped by four white cupolas, which can be entered on each of its four sides. In its day, it was reserved for the most senior high officials. What look like the finest of woodcarvings are, in fact, the finest of stone carvings. The visual effect is of warmth, as the building inside and out is a soft brushed red colour. The ground floor is an open space with a single 6 metre (20 foot) column rising from the centre. This in itself is an irreplaceable work of art. The first two-thirds is heavily carved with five distinct and equally beautiful patterns. As the column rises to support the suspended walkways leading to the centre of the second floor, the carvings expand into five successively greater rings, each of even more ornate decoration. Such a degree of engineering is phenomenal. The second floor has a central space above the column where Akbar was seated. His senior ministers were seated in a circular fashion around the balcony and could approach Akbar along the four walkways leading to the centre. The windows and half walls of the walkways were carved in lace-like patterns to allow cool breezes to pass through. Just one 'window' is a miracle of its own: the 1 by 2-metre (3 by 6 foot) panels are totally carved in stone and fashioned in open flower designs and asymmetrical squares.

The Palace of Honour is the tomb for Salim Chisti, the holy man who predicted the birth of Akbar's sons. The facade of chaste white marble sits off centre in a great red sandstone courtyard. It is built in an ornate style with delicate filigrees and cupolas piercing the cobalt blue sky above it. Women from all over India come here to pray for the birth of a son. Near the tomb a message reads, 'Jesus, Son of Mary (on whom be peace), said: The world is a bridge, pass over it but build no hope upon it. Who hopes for an hour, hopes for eternity. The world is an hour. Spend it in prayer, for the rest is unseen.' On a wall not far away is the unmistakable symbol of the Star of David.

In this inspiring complex many buildings, bathhouses, palaces and temples are interwoven with great stone courtyards. Around the walls are carved stone rings placed 3 metres (10 feet) apart. When large gatherings were held, they could attach brocaded awnings so that Akbar's frequent guests could have shade as they walked about in the delicate Persian style gardens. Formal rows of cypress trees flanked square gardens of flowers, where roses, marigolds, poppies, carnations, and of course, tulips grew in abundance. Akbar loved the sensuality of lush green gardens. Fatehpur Sikri was well known for its bounteous groves of oranges, mangos, apples, coconuts, figs and bananas. Green parakeets faltered and fluttered, the air filled with the sweet rising perfume of incense.

The Golden Abode which was one of the palaces closest to Akbar's heart: belonged to the princess from Amber. Upon her marriage she was given a new name and was called Mariam Zamani. Akbar, always sensitive to the needs of others, built for his Rajput princess apartments designed to make her as happy as possible. The emperor's builders devised little niches and carved columns in the Hindu style to delight her and lessen the sorrow of leaving her former home. Beautiful paintings and fine rugs adorned the walls and ceilings. Her clothing was made from the finest brocades and embroideries. Here she could worship her own Hindu gods and her compassionate and tender king Akbar. Years later, long after the princess died, her great-great-grandson, a born-again Moslem heretic, tried to destroy everything in the Golden Abode. He slashed through the paintings and made rubble of the little clay images. The one thing he could not do was to erase the Hindu blood from his veins.

For each of his other wives, Akbar did the same, making their apartments to suit their religions. Besides his numerous wives he had as many as 800 concubines, housed at the harem serai. Even these places were thoughtfully and carefully constructed, with delicate, hand-carved screens that allowed the ladies to walk down to the cool lake without being seen. These women were not necessarily for Akbar's bed but were more probably entertainers, dancing women and singers of the court.

Akbar's bedchamber was like a cellar. And, like his grandfather Babur, he had a sharp dislike for the humid, sultry heat of India. Streams of water cooled the room, running in specially constructed channels surrounding the walls. The ceiling was a flat stone as big as a table. Everything was designed to keep the room like a deep, cool cave.

Akbar was a generous man who gave away huge sums of money, especially to the poor. As a Jesuit missionary noticed, while observing Akbar in the act of receiving gifts from the poor, '....their little offerings he used to accept with such a pleased look, handling them and putting them to his bosom, as he did not do with most of the lavish gifts of the nobles'.

Why in 1586, after only 14 years, did Akbar abandon his prized Fatehpur Sikri? The most common reason given is a lack of water. Still, there had been provision for water. An artificial lake with a complex series of reservoirs and Persian water wheels had been created and should have been enough for a continuous supply. The answer is more likely to have been fighting. For 14 years he made his base at Lahore owing to a rebellion in Afghanistan. Perhaps he never expected to be away for so long. Perhaps, in later life, his heart was too grievously wounded. His first-born son Jahangir, the child responsible for the construction of Fatehpur Sikri, was so impatient for his father's death that he killed Akbar's dearest friend, Abu-l Fazl, the court historian.

In his last days, spent at Agra, Akbar wandered the courts while his children argued over the throne. It has been officially recorded that he died of dysentery. As his few close friends gathered at his bedside, those who held his trembling hand surely must have wondered if his own son had poisoned him. Before his death an effort was made to convert him back to Islam. It failed. He passed away without prayers, without proper mourners. His children were all too anxious to divide their father's kingdom, to be grief-stricken for too long. For the most honourable and the most conscientious of all the rulers that Asia had ever known, it was a grievous ending.

Chapter 8

Agra

OUR DRIVER WAITED IN the parking lot talking with the other drivers. Identical white bubble-like Ambassador cars sat like giant mushrooms in a red field of stone. Children in scant clothing played a game of tag, stopping when the tourists came along; then the tourists became the game. The three of us sat in silence, thinking melancholy thoughts about Fatehpur Sikri as we drove on toward Agra. But soon the realisation that we were nearing the Taj Mahal began to tease our imagination. Could it live up to what we had just seen? So many people said it was out of this world. What if it wasn't and didn't live up to our expectations? We felt impatient to be there.

I thought a city as famous as Agra would have modern buildings, but there were no department stores and no supermarkets in this vast city which was once the capital of India. The only modern buildings I could see were the hotels and there were plenty of those. Selecting accommodation can be very difficult and it pays to have a good look around. It is impossible to generalise about tariffs and conditions: standards and prices change as soon as a travel guide describes the hotel as 'a bargain and clean'. We went looking for the hotel highly recommended by a reputable, and up-to-date, travel book, but the room prices had already changed. We decided to have a look anyway. The room was large enough but old-fashioned and dowdy. We thanked them and started to leave. 'What price would we be looking for? It is possible we might have something for you at our sister hotel. We are being very sure you will be liking it.' I doubted it.

'We are having a new hotel down the street. It is having the very same name but it is being very new.' The situation, as usual, was starting to get confusing. The three of us got back into the car and drove one block down the street. 'May we have a look? The staff at your sister hotel, the Amar, has sent us here.'

'Oh, certainly, sir, ma'am. They have been calling us. We have a very fine hotel, it is new, new.' Pride was busting their buttons.

Indeed it was brand-new but the room was small and it was still reasonably expensive. 'We are so sorry . . . '

'And what will be being wrong, sir?' We are offering our best to you,' said in the most sad and disappointed voice.

Like cowards we didn't want to say we couldn't afford it, so we said we were sorry but the room was a little too small.

'We have better room, big room and it will be facing the street.'

So we trudged off with all our baggage to the bigger room, feeling guilty because the size of the room was not really the issue. 'You like? Very, very nice room all modern, new.' Indeed, it was new and I looked at it longingly.

'We are really sorry but we cannot afford 1200 rupees.'

'How many rupees can you give?' What a question. If only we had had a quick course in acting, preferably tragic, before we made this trip. We had the feeling that whatever we offered would be seriously considered but didn't want to insult them. We settled on 800 rupees (US$19) and 10 per cent off all meals in the hotel – the new and the old – and the use of the swimming pool at the other hotel. We revelled in the big, clean room, the thick, white towels, the shower that gushed hot water any time of the day and a real double bed. Perhaps best of all, there was a TV set, which not only worked but received CNN and the BBC. After a month on the road we could catch up on the international news in English. The TV soap, *The Bold and the Beautiful*, was greatly improved, I thought, by being spoken in Hindi. Bollywood by the bucketful appeared on every channel. Some commercials had tall blonde women washing their squeaky-clean hair in marble bathrooms and others preparing instant meals in gourmet kitchens. I wondered how it related to the reality of 65 per cent of women in India? How did it make them feel? Hopeful about the future or helpless in their own? In the restaurant the proud, uniformed manager invited us into the kitchen and showed us around, pointing out how clean it was. We were invited to inspect the stove and look at all the shining new pots and pans. The desk manager and the doorman treated us to smiles and tiny bows whenever we came in or went out. A large sign at the hotel desk stated plainly that 1200 rupees was the price for the cheapest room. Certainly an occupied room is better than an empty one. Perhaps they were eager to have us stay because we were older and, in their eyes, respectable, a drawcard for similar foreign tourists. Presumably the local people paid less then the overseas tourists and we still paid too much, but whatever the reasons, the staff made us feel more than welcome. It was a joy to stay at the New Amar Niwas.

We arranged with Dinesh to pick us up at 5 p.m. to go to the Taj Mahal. We put our things away, showered and rested for an hour. I decided this was the occasion to wear a sari so I picked out a blue silk one with a wide gold thread border. I couldn't wear the magnificent orange creation from Jaipur. That would have been definitely overkill. I was nervous enough, appearing for the first time in traditional Indian dress. Could I put it on correctly? I couldn't ask anyone in the hotel to help me because they were all men. Why should I want to do this? It was simple. I was tired of looking so ordinary in my regulation-tourist-sensible-but-dull clothes. I wanted to dress up and in a way that showed respect to the memory of Mumtaz and Shah Jehan. I felt excited about seeing the greatest shrine ever built in the name of love.

Shah Jehan was the son of Jehangir and the grandson of Akbar. Some people might think of Shah Jehan as a schmaltzy over-the-top romantic, so besotted with love that his only claim to fame was a marble tomb for his wife Mumtaz. He was far more than that. As a young man Jehan and his father got on very well together. They fought huge battles together, went through some massacres deluxe and had some successes. But after a while, Jehan got big-headed and thought he could do a better job than his father. Jehangir's reaction was swift and merciless, and Shah Jehan wound up having to hide himself for many years in the lower regions of the Deccan. When Johangir died in 1622, Shah Jehan couldn't get to Agra fast enough. He immediately seized the throne and proclaimed himself emperor. As soon as he arrived, he knew that he was going to have problems with his younger brothers. So, without so much as a beg your pardon, he killed them all. Having done this, he achieved a measure of peace

A Brush with India

and settled down, in the manner of his father before him. He spent extravagant sums of money with wilful and dedicated self-indulgence. He had an extremely bad temper, which he inherited from his father, and an inborn sense of cruelty. He was not interested in being religiously tolerant. All the concerns and progress for religious freedom created by his grandfather Akbar, were completely obliterated. Jehan went on a rampage of outrageous and stupendous spending. He replaced the religious indifference of his father Jehangir, with a full return to Islam. Why? Taxes. He needed the head tax on all non-Moslems and other religious-based taxes to pay for his burgeoning architectural portfolio. He decided the Christians were a bunch of weirdos and had to go. Mumtaz didn't like them either and as a result the Christian church Akbar had let the Jesuits build in Agra was completely destroyed. Naturally, the total plunder and destruction of Hindu religious shrines was a normal extension of Jehan's cruelties and revenue.

Shah Jehan was, like his ancestors, an all-powerful, brutal warrior with formidable responsibilities. He could have lain around on his Persian carpets and let the world go by, but he had a staggering, almost supernatural, appreciation of art and particularly architecture. Under his leadership, throughout the next 30 years of government, he gave India its highest moments of affluence and prestige. Typically and fortuitously, with imperial disregard for cost, he created the finest architecture India has ever known.

When Shah Jehan was 21, he married the niece of his mother, Nur Jehan. Her given name was Arjumand Banu Begam. Her married name was Mumtaz Mahal, or 'Ornament of the Palace.' She was not his first wife but she was his favourite. Sometimes she has been rather unkindly referred to as the Horizontal Queen. In the 17 years of their marriage she gave birth to 14 children. Shah Jehan loved her above all other women, which is particularly compelling because, before his wedding, he was known as a vociferous womaniser. He took Mumtaz everywhere; she was always by his side. He even took her with him in times of battle and uprisings. She was with him in the Deccan, in a tent in the desert, when she gave birth to their last child. From the start, her servant knew the birth was not going well. She sent immediately for Shah Jehan who

Agra

arrived in time to hold her in his arms. They looked at each other for the last time, then she closed her eyes and quietly died. For the husband she left behind, who had everything to live for, including the greatest wealth in the world and vast armies of loyal and savage warriors, her death had rendered all life meaningless. The passing of one fragile woman brought a grievous silence to the plains of India.

Mumtaz died on 28 June 1631. She was 39 years old. Her body, according to Moslem custom, was quickly laid in a temporary grave. A short time later Prince Shuja and a maidservant who had been one of Mumtaz's favourites took her to Agra. Once more her body was laid in a temporary place, this time a garden. On the first anniversary of her death, a great feast was held in her honour. According to the Koran, a woman who dies in childbirth is considered a martyr and her tomb a place of pilgrimage. Work began on her final resting-place, the Taj Mahal, in 1632.

Dinesh approved of my sari. He never talked much but having seen him every day for almost a month, I could tell when he was pleased. This seemed a good sign; at least I was not making a complete fool of myself. Gaston, as I hoped, liked the change and that seemed reason enough to wear the blue silk. We drove the short distance from our hotel to a parking site particularly for visitors to the Taj Mahal. We could only inch forward a car length at a time. An enormous craft fair, full of excitement and colour, was happening just where we wanted to park our car. Thousands of cars and people filled every available space. Merchants of all descriptions were trying to make a swift buck. From food sellers to trinket traders they descended on us like flies and a sea of tea-coloured faces besieged our car. Drivers were yelling out furiously. Carts teetered back and forth on the brink of falling over. Souvenir sellers thrust treasures into every available open window. We finally found a spot eight blocks from the entrance to the Taj Mahal. Dinesh did some fine-tuned manoeuvring to get the car into a minuscule space. Cars are not allowed to go any closer to the Taj and visitors must walk or ride in a rickshaw to the main gate. Before we got one foot out of the car, a rickshaw driver pulled alongside. In a rush we jumped onto the impossibly thin and hard-backed seat of the rickshaw. I was not used to the skirts of the sari and it caught between my legs, threatening to come loose. The rickshaw wallah gave us a big grin and we were off down the road. We crisscrossed our way through the thousands of people who were coming from or going to the fair or the Taj Mahal. A carnival feeling filled the air, along with the intense sweet smell of curry from a myriad of cart wallahs. Food and drink of every description was flung under our noses.

Infinite replicas of the Taj Mahal in every conceivable form were dangled in front of our eyes. I liked one in a blue velvet box only about 12 centimetres (5 inches) in size. With a flip of nimble brown fingers, the sides were folded outwards and up rose a well-fashioned duplicate of the Taj Mahal in white marble, probably plastic. More touts thrust postcards and film into our hands, pleading and begging us to buy. Our rickshaw chauffeur was having none of it. He beat them off with his vocal whip, an unimaginably fierce tirade of Hindi. We rode on a six-block mission to Mumtaz. My sari turned out to be a major attraction, although I couldn't decide if it was approval or I looked a complete idiot. Calls of, 'Sari! Sari!' rang out and, more reassuringly, 'Bu-tee-full'. The women smiled, giggled and covered their mouths with their henna-painted hands. I was worried – did I have it on right? – but the important and looming anxiety was that, if I didn't place my feet just right as I descended from the rickshaw, and the hem got caught in my sandals, the whole thing was going to fall off.

But all was well when we finally arrived at the entrance and paid our man, who insisted on waiting to take us back: he knew then he would be assured of the return fare. I guessed we wouldn't be too hard to locate. We paid the entrance fee and stepped through the high, red, wooden gates. We couldn't see the Taj Mahal yet but walked down a wide walkway amid large and pleasant gardens. The final entrance is a high battlement: a red sandstone gateway topped with 22 cupolas to designate the number of years spent on the building's construction. We waited in line to cross through the final gate. Here there was a security check where food and cigarettes were confiscated. Everyone chewing paan was made to spit the thick gluey paste into a heavily red-stained bucket. It was already three-quarters full.

After all we had been told, the photos we had seen, the books we had read, we were not prepared for the first impression. The sight of the Taj Mahal passed through our senses like a gentle and intoxicating kiss. In the late afternoon, with the sun just starting to descend, we were warmly enticed forward towards the high marble platform of the tomb. It appeared serene, perfectly proportioned and charismatically feminine. Peace settled around our shoulders like an invisible cloak. We reached out to hold each other's hand. No woman in all history has had a finer monument built to her memory.

Long stretches of reflective pools, grass and cypresses, flank walkways that lead to the steps of the final resting-place of Mumtaz. We removed our shoes, as everyone must before ascending. At the top of the stairs, the supremely beautiful entrance to the tomb beckoned. The mausoleum has 12 sides and four are entrances. The roof is a massive spired dome. When it was first built there were silver gates at the entrance but their absence is not missed. Inlaid in the walls are thousands of inscriptions from the Koran, one of which invites those who are ' pure of heart' to 'enter the gardens of Paradise'. We stepped inside. An octagonal screen of sublime beauty gave privacy and poignancy to the two tombs lying side by side. If God had decided to add his personal contribution, His handiwork, it would have been the screen that shelters these two lovers, which took more than 10 years to create. Made of the finest, transparent alabaster marble, it looks like fine lace; each section is carved from one solid block. It is poignant to see Mumtaz's coffin in the centre of the great overhead dome. Her husband's matching coffin, larger, is by her side. Their actual remains are directly below in an earthly crypt, a common practice in large tombs. The 99 names of Allah are inscribed on Mumtaz's gravestone. Gardens of exquisite flowers cut in inlaid marble adorn her marble crypt. Curling petals and leaves, which glisten with the shine of semi-precious stones, decorate the surface. Blood red poppies rise and stretch, together with tiny buds, promising to burst from pods that are 400 years old. Yellow stone lilies, with golden threaded stamens and green leaves of six or seven shades, turn in the light as if blown by a soft desert breeze. Along the edges of her tomb are bouquets and bowers of feathery cream blossoms, wrought from solid white marble. This is a love story written in stone, an eternal reminder that love between a man and a woman is the finest gift of life. This is, too, a lasting statement that human potential can be expressed in a form that transforms it from mortal to immortal.

The next morning, three weeks after Gaston fell ill, he finally felt strong enough to go back to painting. We talked in bed about where he might go but when I got up to pull back the curtains from our windows it was raining, our first day of bad weather. Never in all the years of our painting trips had we had such bad luck. What was it about this trip? It is not easy to get a collection of paintings together. The weather conditions have to be right and the artist has to be motivated and physically strong. This was not the first time we had experienced problems. Stricken by a kidney stone attack, Gaston had lain feverish with desperate pain in a camping ground in the south of France. Another time he had an unexpected hernia problem and carrying the painting box became impossible. I could carry the box but I couldn't do the painting. By lying on the ground and resting every 20 minutes he managed to get through his work. Also in France, we returned to our tent after a superb dinner, to find our sleeping bags floating in 60 centimetres of floodwater. There are always obstacles but in the end we have the paintings. This was the first time we would be going home without achieving what we had come for. Since it was raining, we decided to drive around and do the essential, time-consuming work of finding some possible painting sites. No one can help Gaston find what he is looking for. I know roughly what subject he wants but that is only one part of what appeals to him: he is also looking for colour and light. Early morning or late afternoons are the best times for light and shadow. Also, unless the subject has a harmonious colour, he isn't interested.

The city of Agra has a population of 1,200,000. After the Taj Mahal, our visit to Kinari Bazaar, the old marketplace, was bewildering. The Taj Mahal was a pristine and beautifully immaculate world; the bazaar was awash with black, sticky mud. There was not a department store to be seen. Instead, there were thousands of little cubby-holes, which sold individual items. We walked around the market in the rain, flabbergasted at the array of shopkeepers. There were ironworkers, coppersmiths and tinsmiths all working in a clash of metallic tunes. There were flower stalls with mountains of marigolds and wreaths for the recently dead. Tea merchants sold black tea, green tea, jars of tea and bundles of tea. I admired lovely lengths of material, but some were so garish they made me giggle. Cloth merchants abounded. There were so many bolts of material they could have paved the whole city of Agra. Barbers perched on tiny wooden platforms, with scissors snipping, cutting hair in the drizzling rain. Hooked hanging carcasses of freshly killed animals hung like surreal elongated statues. Huge shining cleavers flashed, reducing the hanging sculptures to bloody shreds. Scavengers squatted in doorways. Moslem women hid behind burkhas and Indian women covered their heads with their saris. Turbans bobbed about, making the bazaar seem like a patchwork quilt. Cars honked and cluttered the narrow lanes; rickshaws and bicycles skidded in the mud. Sluggish camel and bullock carts pushed, groaned and grunted their way through the crowds to deliver goods. Bottles, rags and newspapers filled the scroungers' burlap sacks. Even they had their place in this world of commerce. Car exhausts, foraging hands, people spitting and animals defecating were things to be mindful of.

Agra is a beehive, a city of workers, rich and poor. The emperors, the Mogul kings, have long gone. Even the former maharaja, though revered, is not often mentioned. They have all left behind their monuments and their palaces but not much more. Most of their descendants speak Hindi. Some speak English, which comes in four categories: British English, some English, English that is completely unrecognisable as English, and lastly, the person who doesn't speak English but knows someone who does. The Taj Mahal and Agra Fort are for the tourists and better-off Indians who can afford the gate fee. The regal buildings of the Great Fort are bereft of their former splendour; long ago stripped by succeeding invaders.

We crossed the Yamuna River bridge to see if we could find a vantage point opposite the Taj Mahal. It was crammed with cars, trucks and pedestrians. I looked in vain for a sign that would mention the maximum weight allowed, then crossed

A Brush with India

my fingers and studied the knobbly knees of the camels and the bending axles of burdening trucks as they glided past our windows. We found there was no road to take us opposite the Taj Mahal. On the other side there were only fields and sandbanks, and private land. Walking in the pouring rain was not an option for someone just out of his sickbed so we braved the road back to the Taj Mahal and, with a little bribery, managed to drive to the front gate. We drove further to the southern end where the only way down to the river is by foot. Luckily the rain stopped and Gaston found an Indian guide who walked down with him to the riverbank, this time on the same side as the Taj Mahal. I stayed in the car with Dinesh.

A snake charmer ambled over and, with a crooked smile, set up his one-man, two-snake and one-flute exhibition. I paid no attention. I looked in the other direction. Thinking I couldn't see properly, he moved closer. The snakes' flattened heads reared up and slid along the windowpane, their ball-bearing eyes looking for prey. Dinesh, trying to comfort me, said the snakes had their teeth cut off so they could not bite. I understood this turbaned charmer and his two slithering sidekicks were only trying to make a living but I turned away, a coward, and a miserly one. Gaston came back to the car, exhausted and ready to return to our hotel. He had found a boatman willing to take him to the other side of the river. If he decided to return, he would need to walk about a mile down to the river, gingerly cross a sandbar and get into a boat. After lifting and lugging his heavy paintbox in and out of the boat he would need a further walk to find a suitable painting spot. And the whimsical factors of rain, wind or cloud were always a possibility.

In the afternoon I went shopping with Dinesh. I felt I almost owed it to him after breaking my promise to him in Jaipur. A few doors along from our hotel was Raman Exports. I am not the dream shopper that merchants stay awake at nights praying for. I like to look, make comparisons and think for a while before I buy anything. After so many years of travelling, we don't bring home souvenirs. Gaston always tells me to go ahead and buy what I want as long as I can wear it on my ears or eat it. The only other thing we might consider is a rug, a small carpet unique to the country we have visited. Since we would

Agra

not have a car after we left Agra, I was not considering buying one. Carrying a rug around would have been ludicrous.

Mr R. Tandon of Raman Exports was very understanding. 'Would ma'am like to see the rugs?'

'No, no, I just want to look at a few saris and perhaps something small for a child.'

'It will not be taking much of ma'am's time. You do not need to buy. I assure you. It is of no importance. What matters is to see how hard our people are working and the beautiful carpets their hands are doing. Just behind the showroom, you will see. This will be being of great interest for you.'

Mr R. Tandon was a very dignified older man. While I guessed he had an ulterior motive – 'no importance' indeed – so did I. Here was a well-educated gentleman with whom I could discuss the life and times of things Indian. In any case, there was no way I was going to buy a rug.

'We will just be walking.'

And yes, at the back of the store a young man worked patiently working at a loom. The paper patterns lay on his left and while his right hand wove the matching colours, his left hand brought down the top of the loom to make less than 3 millimetres (1/8 inch) of pattern. It was a long tedious job, requiring colossal patience brought about by many years of practice. I wondered if he had learnt his craft as a child and was now the showpiece for the tourists. Despite the Child Labour Prohibition Act of 1986 there are still hundreds of thousands of children employed in the carpet-weaving industry in India. Little fingers are ideal for weaving ... and weaving, and weaving. An eight-hour day would be a vacation.

India produces more carpets than Iran. Mr R. Tandon led me to his showroom. I still protested I didn't want to buy and he still said he only wanted to show me. He knew. He knew that once I saw the rugs, if nothing else, I would have to admire their quality and their designs. I felt confident, in control and firm that I would not buy. The rugs were drop-dead gorgeous.

'I absolutely love them but I can't carry them.'

'No problem, we mail.' A country like India? Could I hand over a large sum of money and just expect the rug to arrive at my doorstep? How much would I have to pay for customs duty? These were things I should have thought about before I left. The design and colour of the rug I wanted would have to be custom made. It would take three months before he could send it – time enough for my Visa payment to be long gone. I knew my credit card would be charged today and not the day the carpet was mailed. I reminded myself that the transaction with my credit card would have to be done in front of me, not carried away to the back of the shop and returned for me to sign. Mr R. Tandon showed me dozens of cotton-wrapped parcels, ready to be shipped around the world. Presumably others had found the courage to trust him. He reminded me of how much I would be helping the poor rug makers of India. Tiny nimble fingers came to mind, although we had not spoken of the unspeakable. I reminded him about Dinesh and how I hoped he would think of him also. I took the chance. I told him if he saw me with my husband, not to mention the carpet. I wanted it to be a surprise for our wedding anniversary. Mr R. Tandon and I knew my husband would think I was crazy. Unspoken matters.

A few days later, when we were walking in the street, Mr R. Tandon called out, saying he wanted to meet my husband. I held my breath. But it seemed that Dinesh had been bragging to the entire populace of Agra about his tourist-wallah who was a famous artist and he only wanted to say hello. Three months later, a grubby, well-travelled white linen parcel arrived on our doorstep. Inside, carefully, intricately, folded was the rug I had requested. It was beautiful. A message inside from Mr R. Tandon said that he hoped we liked it and asked if we could please let him know that it had arrived safely.

It would be very unwise to say that all rug dealers are as honest as Raman Exports but this is true anywhere. The rug we bought was new, not as old and valuable as you can buy from Iran, Baluchistan or Kashmir. Rug making in India only began in the 16th century when Persian weavers were brought in by Akbar to teach the locals. The art of picking the right rug, perhaps a valuable rug, is a complete study of its own. I keep to a set amount, never over US$300. I know little about the subject, so the wisest thing for me to do is to pick something that will be a joy to look at, and a reminder of the country we visited.

Agra

It was still raining the next day. We couldn't change the weather so we decided to go sightseeing. The most interesting thing to see in Agra, aside from the Taj Mahal, is Agra Fort. Akbar began its construction in 1565. The towering, circling walls are 27 metres (90 feet) high and, in some places, almost 11 metres (35 feet) thick. The outer wall, which is several kilometres long, was originally covered in a plaster made from egg whites and lime. Hundred of the thousands of eggs were used to make it rainproof and to provide a glossy sheen. The entrance gates are soaring wooden structures with iron embedded spikes to discourage enemy invaders and their pachyderms. The fort is run down but it is easy to see how magnificent it once was.

In 1628, after the death of his father Jahangir, Shah Jehan was formally enthroned. He became India's greatest Mogul emperor. He never came close or even wanted the title of greatest humanitarian, like his grandfather Akbar, but he did command the largest territory, had the most power and the most wealth. Underground, hidden at Agra Fort were two vaults, each 6.5 metres (22 feet) square and 9 metres (30 feet) high. One vault was filled with gold, the other with silver. Ninety-seven per cent of the population made daily tax contributions to Shah Jehan's colossal spending.

Disregarding his grandfather's supreme efforts as the first builder of Agra Fort, Shah Jehan had almost everything but the outer wall destroyed. Nearly 500 fine red sandstone buildings built by Akbar were torn down. The famous Peacock Throne, one of the most outstanding objects commissioned by Shah Jehan, is no longer at the fort. It took seven years to construct and cost millions of rupees. A French jeweller who had seen the throne described it as solid gold, covered by a canopy studded with gems and set off by pearls. At the top a peacock was fashioned in blue sapphires with a body of gold. A huge ruby hung at its breast with a pearl at its centre weighing at least 50 carats. He counted 108 rubies and 116 emeralds of the finest quality. The 12 columns that supported the canopy were completely covered with fine pearls. One hundred and fifty years later, when invaders rampaged through the palace in Delhi from which the throne had been removed, it was smashed into smaller pieces and carted off.

The sense that one gets in visiting the fort is not so much of the fine buildings, because they have been badly damaged by Persians, Jats and the English in successive generations, but the grandeur of its enormous size. It was a complete city of its own. People living on the outside only saw the emperor on his return journeys from forays into the Deccan. The spectacle of his homecoming must have been enough to convince anyone that he was a mighty, godlike ruler. As far as the eye could see, the earth would have been covered in a solid mass of people as endless columns of camels, elephants with howdahs and armies of soldiers on horseback, their long spears shining in the sun, rode proudly behind their warrior king. Brilliantly coloured flags and banners proclaimed him their conquering emperor. Twenty drawn coaches for Shah Jehan's personal use led the procession but he preferred to ride into Agra on his magnificent dark grey horse with the highest amirs and princes close behind. There were so many elephants the ground shook and trembled with their weight. At the gate of the fort warriors dismounted and walked up the wide gateways. Only Shah Jehan and his sons were permitted to enter Agra Fort on horseback.

Life inside the fort was equally flamboyant. On Thursday public sentences of the condemned were carried out. On other days the emperor would gather his court round him to watch the phenomenon of elephant fighting. From the safety of the ramparts they looked down on the river to watch pairs of combat elephants, each with its own special rider. This spectacle was always performed in the river, as it was the only way to bring the enraged animals under control once the contest was over. An obstruction, such as a mud wall, was constructed in the water. The winner of the contest was the first elephant to succeed in demolishing the wall and routing out the other opponent. The bigger, more powerful bull elephants were selected for the fights; they were then systematically tormented and stabbed until they were completely out of control and ready to annihilate anything. The riders, often tossed off in this horrific arena, were trampled to death. But for the one who won, the prize money was excellent. If a rider died, the emperor provided for his family for the rest of their lives.

Agra

But Agra Fort holds in its memory many beautiful things as well. In the zenana the women of Shah Jehan enjoyed a luxurious existence. Although he had Mumtaz as his favourite, it was still *de rigueur* for the king to have large numbers of women at his disposal. The wives and consorts sheltered behind walls, hidden from the eyes of other men, where they freely enjoyed each other's company in the beautifully constructed gardens. The large marble swimming pool had built-in carved marble armchairs for comfort. The ones that were still totally intact looked appealing and inviting. The Grape Garden, the Anguri Bagh, was part of the zenana. Contrary to its name, no living fruit entwined itself on its stone pergola. Instead, there was a latticework of emeralds and rubies representing the green and red of grapes, and the vines twisted and turned with the sheen of the gold from which they were made. During the day flowers of all varieties filled hundreds of containers. Today, feathery, purple nemesia and feral bulbs grow in scraggly survival where once they were living carpets. Machchi Bhawan, the Fish Square, an immaculately attended pool, was once filled with exotic, sacred fish for the pleasure of the court. The sounds of flowing water culminating in elaborate and numerous waterfalls cooled the fever of hot days. At night, the palace was a world of soft flickering light from thousands of oil lamps.

The saddest and most beautiful place within the fort is the Jasmine Tower. In 1658, the emperor's oldest son, Aurangzeb, deposed his father and locked him away in this ivory jail. Shah Jehan lived here for 11 years. Every day he sat looking directly across to the Taj Mahal, knowing he would soon lie beside the woman he had loved so much. Humbled by imprisonment, he thought of little else than their life together. In his last years, the memory of Mumtaz, and the sight of her resting-place, must have been his daily comfort.

We felt exhausted after walking around Agra Fort. We needed some serious sustenance and to cheer ourselves up because it was still raining. The day before we had gone looking for hotels, more specifically restaurants in hotels. It seemed so long since we had seen anything other than Indian food. Gaston needed what he calls 'real food' – food cooked in the French style, preferable by French chefs. Justifiably, the

French have a reputation for the finest cuisine but have you ever noticed how a Francophile will make the most incredibly biased remarks about food from other countries? For instance, 'The food in India would be all right if they just wouldn't put spices in it.' Or at a Thai restaurant, 'It's great, but it's too hot, the vegetables aren't cooked, there's no sauce and where are the potatoes?'

For the first time since our arrival in India Gaston ate enthusiastically. Greedily, but politely, with little time for conversation, he consumed sole meunière served with pan-fried, well-cooked beans and carrots and lots of scalloped potatoes. I could hardly believe we could order a great thick steak, 'grilled to your liking and served with your choice of sauce, green or black peppercorn or beurre Maitre d'hôtel'. I toyed with the idea of ordering and watching our waiter as he placed on the table, a hunk of rare, bloody 'mother cow'.

Although Agra is not in Rajasthan, most people here are also vegetarians. There are five reasons why a Hindu is a vegetarian: one, the Dharmic Law or Ahimsa, the law of non-injury to living creatures; two, the Karmic Consequence, which says that, by inflicting injury, pain or death, even indirectly by eating other creatures, one must in the future experience the same suffering in equal measure; three, the Spiritual reason: food determines the body's chemistry and what we eat affects our consciousness and thoughts. To live in a state of higher consciousness in peace, love and happiness for all creatures, one cannot eat meat, fish, shellfish, fowl or eggs. By ingesting these creatures, anger, jealousy, anxiety, suspicion and, of course, the fear of death, which are locked into the flesh of butchered creatures, are in turn manifested in the person who eats them. The fourth reason concerns health. A vegetarian diet is easier to digest and still provides a wide range of nutrients. Eating meat imposes an extra burden on the digestive system by adding impurities to the body. And number five is the ecological reason. The loss of species, the destruction of rainforests to create farmland, the loss of topsoil and pollution of water and air are all by-products of meat eating in the human diet.

Not everyone in India is vegetarian, far from it. The two cultures that have influenced the food most are the Hindu and the Moslem but the Portuguese, the Persians and the British also made important contributions. A lot of Hindus eat meat today as do the Christians and the Moslems. The essence of good Indian cooking revolves around the appropriate use of herbs and spices. The skill lies in their subtle blending so that they enhance rather than overwhelm the flavour of a dish. Besides spices, some other main ingredients are milk products such as ghee and yoghurt. (Ghee is unsalted butter simmered until the sediment turns golden. It is then strained and poured into a container.) Lentils (dals) are also common ingredients in the Indian diet. The differences between the various foods come from the types of religion practised and the varying nationalities.

Rajasthan has its own traditional specialties and culture concerning food. The tradition of Rajasthani cooking is very old and elaborate. Because of the people's warlike lifestyle and the lack of availability of products in the desert, food evolved to fit the conditions. Of necessity, food that could last for several days and did not have to be heated was preferred. Lack of water and green vegetables also had their effect: it is therefore logical to find an abundance of such dishes as lentils, dried fruits and nuts. Curries are made with potatoes and desert beans with funky names like mogri and sangri. The Rajput tradition included meat: chicken, venison, peacock, quail, duck and wild boar were well known. It is very important to try and understand what the names mean on a menu. Otherwise, unless you are staying in a foreign tourist hotel and paying five times more than in an Indian hotel, you will wind up eating curried spinach from Monday to Sunday. You will lose weight and, worse, you will become uninterested in eating. This is a terrible loss of opportunity. Indian food is a wonderful culinary experience and a varied one. It is said the really good Indian cooking is to be found in the home. The dinner we had in Bikaner made by the wife of the hotel owner was a good example. It was not overly spicy or harsh, or worse, imitation Western. The home kitchen is one area in which women have their say: it is their world and their source of pride. It is very rare to see a woman working in a hotel, a restaurant or even a women's clothing shop. Most women stay at home. Only higher class Indian woman have a free life.

I liked eating the local food although I was ignorant about the meaning of the names on the menus. It was my great loss in Rajasthan, for when we got to Agra, I had some absolutely delicious meals. While Gaston was eating his, 'Continental Favourites', I had things like gosht ya murgh ki biryani, a tender aromatic blend of lamb, slowly cooked with basmati rice, herbs and spices. My favourite dessert was gulab-jamuns, small fried balls of custard in a warm sauce. It would be worth a return trip to Agra just to eat that again.

All over India the culture of food differs, just as it does in France: the various areas have their own specialties. Generally speaking, the Sikhs of the Punjab and the Hindu of Rajasthan are vegetarian. Wherever Moslems are, you will find non-vegetarian menus, as they are called. Meat forms a large part of their diet, including beef. The Jains are not only vegetarians but do not eat beetroot or tomatoes because they have the colour of blood. They also do not eat root vegetables since pulling them out of the earth might cause an innocent insect to lose its life. Southern Indians, in the area where the majority of Christians live, prefer to eat food that is roasted or steamed. New Delhi Hindus eat chicken, quail and some other meat.

'Satisfactions' and 'Continental Favourites' are the part of a menu that means Western style food. From a middle-class hotel or restaurant and downwards, order at your own risk. There are usually cutlets of some sort, such as vegetable, chicken or mutton; these are leftovers from the reign of the British. Well, not quite that old, but almost.

After a good dinner many people enjoy paan as it is considered a mild digestive. A concoction of spices and seasonings, it is chewed with betel nut. Paan sellers are everywhere. They carry a collection of containers with various ingredients and either have a permanent shop or walk around with their wares in a box in front of them, like cigarette girls used to do. There are all sorts of variations: plain paan, sweet paan and sometimes even costly opium paan. I admit I didn't try it but my reason was vanity. Chewing paan gives a person a red mouth and teeth. When you have finished with it, you spit the whole thing in a wet, red blob on the pavement. A great big smile from a person who has eaten paan looks like they have just been sharing dinner with vampires. Long-term use results in blackened teeth and addiction to betel nut.

The next morning, after two days of rain and cold, the sun looked as though it might come out. We met Dinesh at eight and even though conditions were not ideal Gaston decided to give it a try anyway. A fine mist filtered through the morning air and spread out over the Jamuna River. It was hard to tell whether it was rain or sulphuric acid. Agra is a heavily polluted area because of the many coke-based industries and the exhausts of so many vehicles. A considerable effort is being made to move these factories from the city because the falling acid, five times higher than the maximum level, is constantly damaging the Taj Mahal. Atmospheric conditions such as mists are not always good for painting because they render the subject flat, without shadows. Gaston set up his easel below the wall of Agra Fort next to the river. The river was low and instead of having shimmering water as a foreground to the subject it was almost a dry riverbed. Neverless it was still a handsome topic with the Taj Mahal in the distance. Dinesh helped Gaston with his heavy paintbox and easel and he set up on a sandbank. There were a few trees and shrubs sheltering him but not blocking the view. It was an area where there were no houses and therefore it was also the local latrine: luckily his gaze was up and distant. This wasn't the first time he had found himself standing in the local privy. (After I had been in India for a while, these sorts of things didn't seem to bother me so much. What is a person supposed to do in a country of one billion people and three toilets?)

Within minutes of squeezing oil paint onto the palette and setting his canvas on the easel, Gaston was surrounded by 15 men and boys. I was surprised at how well dressed his audience was. Most were wearing jeans and sweaters and recently pressed shirts. Many had immaculate white trousers. I admired their ability to be neat when living conditions were often cramped and difficult. They were fascinated: clearly, watching Gaston painting from life was a new experience for them. Impressionism was an art form they did not seem familiar with. They slowly discovered that, if they first looked at the strokes of paint on the canvas and then moved back,

A Brush with India

the subject became strongly visible. The splashes of colour, the paint applied with a wide brush, still managed to produce a recognisable form. The former greatness of Indian artwork relied on very stylised, tight work, painted in painstaking miniature with watercolours on rice paper. Gaston's work was something quite different for them. They were quiet and respectful and didn't stand too close. I had the feeling, knowing the Indian ability to do and try everything, that they were trying to learn in one easy lesson exactly how it was done. I felt encouraged when the painting was finished. It had been 15 days and thousands of kilometres since Gaston's last painting. I cannot think of any other profession that demands so much dedication and makes so few promises of reward.

Dinesh was leaving us and we felt sad to see him go. He had arranged for someone else to complete our last few days with the car. Before he left he helped us to find our rail tickets for Varanasi and New Delhi. When we drove over to the hotel where we were supposed to pick them up they were, of course, nowhere to be found. The hotel wouldn't let us use their phone so we went out, found a phone and called the tourist office at Delhi. It turned out the tickets were at the hotel. It must have been too easy to file them under our names: instead they were addressed to the 'French couple'. We didn't bother asking why.

When we handed Dinesh a white, sealed envelope containing his tip he had the good manners not to rip it open and see how much was in it. A good-looking young man with a small moustache, Dinesh was dressed that day in his navy trousers and shirt and a maroon sweater. The blue baseball cap and dark glasses he wore every day were gifts from previous clients. It would have been nice to give him something similar as a memento. The only thing of ours which we thought he might like was a big blue beach towel with a fanciful Japanese fish pattern. Since his towel had been stolen when we were at Pushkar we hoped he would not be offended if we offered him ours. I wanted to buy him a watch – only a few days before I had realised that he didn't wear one – but since I didn't know where to buy one that would last for more than a few days, I just put something extra in the envelope.

Dinesh was a good person who believed with all his heart

in his religion and his mother. We would have thought something was wrong if we hadn't had incense burning in the car each day. We grew to know exactly what he meant with his expressions of 'Very cheating' or 'No like' and 'Some drivers very crazy' – and, of course, just plain 'Cheaters!' At 22, he was just a boy but with his older brother he helped to support his mother, sister, sister-in-law and the three children of his brother. How he did this on 1200 rupees/US$28 a month, I could not even begin to fathom. Since his father had died, his mother would arrange for a wife for him. According to Dinesh he would have some say in the matter, for instance if he didn't like her picture. They would have a ring ceremony such as I had attended in Jodhpur and six months to a year later they would marry. When I asked him if it was true that he wouldn't see his fiancé in the time between the ring ceremony and the wedding he told me, with a small grin, 'perhaps I could go for a walk with her but I wouldn't tell my mother. She would be very, very angry.' He also told me in a quiet gentle voice how much he loved their summer home. They only lived in Delhi to make enough money to survive. In the hot months, June and July, when there were not many tourists, he went back to his village in the hills: Mayal Bakhag, near Nepal.

I asked Dinesh if he could do or be anything he wanted, what would that be? He wanted to be a farmer in the hills near his home: that was his big dream. His brother had taught him to drive. It was a big secret not to be told to his mother: she had never wanted him to be a driver on the nightmare roads of India. His brother had taught him well but Dinesh seemed too gentle a soul for such a roulette ride of life and death. He had one last confession to make, if I promised not to tell 'sir': he had never been to Rajasthan before and had only driven from Delhi to Agra and back to Delhi. I wasn't too surprised. I admired him even more.

Over the next few days Gaston managed a few more paintings and it started to feel as though we were getting back to the normal swing of our life. Everyone at the hotel continued to be thoughtful and polite. One of the waiters in the dining room asked what perfume I was wearing and I laughed, as I wasn't wearing any: it was Gaston's aftershave. We carefully wrote the name down and the waiter tried in vain

A Brush with India

to find it in the market. On our last morning all the waiters asked to have their picture taken with us; we promised to send the photos when we returned home.

On our last morning in Agra we returned to visit the Taj Mahal for the last time. It was early, there was once again a heavy mist and it was cooler than usual. Our new driver, Sanjay, took us to a different gate, and said it was a short walk from there. But when we entered we were suddenly descended on by rickshaw wallahs who told us it was over a kilometre, 'very long, very long'. and absolutely we should go with one of them. We climbed into a rickshaw and sped down hill, arriving at the gate four small blocks later. We laughed again at ourselves: how naive we still were. Our diminutive rickshaw wallah took it all very seriously and said he would be waiting for us.

In the early morning, in a different light and the mist, the Taj Mahal was a woman dressed in another gown, just as beautiful but dreamy, ethereal. We were moved by the aura of calm, the clear and poignant beauty. It seemed like an architectural masterpiece that had somehow floated down from a cloud in heaven. We looked at the photo galleries; we visited the mosque, that flanks the mausoleum. But each time the shrine was out of sight, we felt impatient to see it again, as if we had only minutes left to share with a lover.

Our rickshaw wallah was waiting for us. With his pencil-thin legs and ragged clothing I easily outweighed him two to one. We got in, then realised the four blocks were uphill so we got out again. We struck a pride-bargain: we agreed to get back into the rickshaw just before the last turn, so the other wallahs would see us arriving in his rickshaw. The total price for the trip down, waiting two hours and returning to the gate was 50 cents. The headman-rickshaw wallah took the money and handed our man less than half.

For the rest of the day we rested, packed our clothes and got ready for our first train experience in India. We had heard all sorts of reports about Indian trains. Most first-class travel experiences we had read about seemed favourable. Agra to Varanasi is nearly 600 kilometres (360 miles) and the idea that we could possibly sleep through a good deal of it appealed to us. But what about the trains? Were they safe? What were the

Agra

sleeping conditions like? We were about to find out.

Our hotel was an hour's drive away from the railway station. (In India, distance is calculated by degree of difficulty in manoeuvring on the road, not by actual length.) Our first drive at night contained all the horrors I have mentioned before but in the darkness it was like racing through an unlit tunnel, objects becoming visible only when they were practically on top of us. Astonishingly, vehicles had either full-beam headlights or no lights at all; dipped lights were practically unheard of and many cars had no tail-lights. Gaston sat in the front seat complaining bitterly about years being taken off his life. The road was jammed with cars and bulky Tata trucks, oxen, camels and carts, bicycles and motorbikes. Many passing animals were taller and bigger than the car. Walls of animal flesh would squash against the windows; big, wide muscles would flex, and nudge the car door. Dinesh had said he was returning to Delhi at night and felt apprehensive and nervous about it. Now, I understood why.

We drove through small villages with Christmas tree lights strung merrily from shop to shop. Feeble electric light and candles shone dimly from inside homes and stores. Business went on just as briskly as in daytime. People walked about doing their shopping and children played in the streets.

The train station at Agra was frenetic. People were running in all directions and taxis and transport of all types manoeuvred back and forth, discharging their passengers and voluminous baggage. Camels squabbled and kicked in the confusion. Carts were strewn everywhere. The building itself looked like Gotham City, Central Station – dark, ominous and forbidding. Long, steep flights of stairs, two storeys high, led up and over the station to the other platforms. I thought of our luggage. How were we going to carry our bags, let alone find what platform we should be on? I need not have worried: as soon as Sanjay stopped the car, a porter descended upon us. He wore a red jacket, white pants and red turban and a copper armband declaring him an official 'coolie' of the station. As our feet touched the ground, he opened the back of the car and was swinging our extra large black suitcase on top of his head. The paintbox followed in the same direction. My backpack was slung over his left shoulder. We had hardly

A Brush with India

said goodbye to our driver before our luggage was winding its way through the crowds.

Pushing hard through the dark, and in a sea of people, I understood how salmon must feel when they are spawning up streams: they know there is somewhere they have to be and they'd had better keep swimming like hell. The coolie ran straight up the steps, smiling and laughing at our feeble efforts to keep up with him. We were wide-eyed, not only because it was so dimly lit, but because we were wondering what we had got ourselves into. We stumbled up the stairs, across the trestles – one, then two – and finally down the stairs. The platform seemed endless. We kept running. Finally, we stopped halfway down the platform. Our baggage was plopped on the ground by a seat, which resembled an old church pew. Bewildered and breathless, we plopped beside the luggage. 'Good job? Many rupee?' Yeah, yeah, we knew the drill and in this case were happy to pay. Some kind stranger from the crowd who spoke English told us that we should pay him only when he had finished the job. He would come back when the train arrived in another hour and get our baggage on board.

We settled down, huddled against one another, with our baggage in a circle around the front of us, pioneer wagon fashion. We were the only Europeans in sight. Life at night, near midnight, on an Indian railway station platform is intimidating. We had been warned to keep our belongings close to us: thieves made an art form out of robbing 'phorens'. It was cold, the coldest it had been in all our time in India: it could have been no more than 10°C(50°F). We could not be absolutely sure we were on the right platform. As our eyes adjusted to the gloomy, low light I noticed a wire cage on our left. It was a holding space for baggage and miscellaneous goods. In front of us was a rusty, unlit, stationary train. Behind us was the other track, which was empty. Glancing again at the wire cage I saw a man sleeping on the concrete about a metre from where I was sitting. His blanket looked thinner than my cotton sweater. I saw policemen walking in pairs, swaggering up and down, disappearing into the murky light. A woman wearing a bright orange sari and white rubber jandals walked to the edge of the platform, squatted beside the empty train and peed on the concrete. A dark pool of urine spread out beneath her. Something touched my arm and I jerked in an uncontrollable reflex: a rag blanket had been the offender. At my feet and along the edge of our chair another soul was making up his bed. Rolled up, his sparse belongings became his pillow. He had already unfolded and stretched out his turban into a sheet and placed it on the ground. A skeleton of a man, he positioned the length of his body around the wooden end of the chair, and his head near my feet. His only other possession, a threadbare grey blanket, he pulled right over him, from his toes to his head. I murmured, 'Goodnight, Mr India.'

While we waited, I began to realise that what I had thought was an empty train in front of us was teeming with passengers. They were sitting in the dark and must have been there for quite some time. I couldn't see any lights at all, not even a candle. I saw people moving about the carriage but how they knew where they were supposed to be was a mystery to me. Were they going to hurtle off into the night with all the lights off? Would our train be the same?

Twenty minutes later Gaston decided he should try and find a station attendant or someone who could reassure us that we were on the right platform. I moved the baggage closer, hoping he would not be too long. I felt some comfort when I saw the two soldiers with rifles: it could have been my imagination or wishful thinking but they seemed to be staying within my sight. Gaston returned after only a few minutes with good and bad news. He had found two foreigners who had their driver and a personal guide with them and discovered that we were in the right place but had no reserved sleeping accommodation on the train. He had to leave again and sort out our sleeping arrangements but this time with the guide. Once again I sat alone with the baggage. It was now after midnight, the train was late and it was getting colder. I watched the chai wallah going up and down, swinging a big teapot back and forth and crying out, 'Chai-tea! Chai-tea!' I was wondering what he used for cups when the question became immaterial because the lights went out. The darkness was complete: the term pitch-black developed a new meaning for me. If anyone wanted to steal our bags, this was going to be the time. Power shortages are a part of daily life in India but here in this place, and so

A Brush with India

late at night, it seemed grotesque. I sat it out, calmly, showing no outward signs of nervousness.

The lights were out for three or four minutes but it seemed much, much longer. As the lights came back on everyone looked and behaved as if nothing had happened. There was no visible sign of relief, no twitter of panic, nothing at all. I was thinking about the subject of heart failure when out of the corner of my eye I saw something large, quick and hairy running toward a discarded plastic bag. It was a rat, a black rat that had come hurtling out from underneath the bench I was sitting on. Instinctively, I lifted my sandalled feet up onto the suitcases. This was no dinky mouse: it was the size of a small cat. Mesmerised. I watched as it left the bag, ran back under the bench and up and over the body of my sleeping sidekick and whisked into the wire cage. I had to keep swallowing the big pools of spit that formed in my mouth as I saw it join its extensive family. They were everywhere.

I was ecstatic to see Gaston returning, especially since he brought back the good news that we 'probably' had a sleeper bed for the night. We didn't join the other couple because they were much further down the platform; it was too hard to move our baggage and we were not sure that the porter would find us. We waited and we waited. Messages in Hindi blurted out over the loudspeaker every few minutes but we, of course, could not understand a word. Just as a young man seated next to us told us the train would be another hour, a train suddenly appeared and with it our porter. He grabbed our things and started to run towards the carriages. The guide who had been with Gaston saw the porter running down the platform and began yelling, 'Idiot! Idiot!' It was the wrong train. An hour later our train finally arrived but this time the porter had no idea what carriage we should be on. The guide came to our rescue again, screaming 'You need to be another 30 carriages further down.' He plunged toward me, grabbed my hand and told me to run. Our porter, with our baggage on top of his head and under his arms, was nowhere to be seen.

Chapter 9

Varanasi

In a flurry of turban, paintbox, copper armband and a wide smile, the porter got us safely onto the train. We were travelling ACI class, which meant a two-tiered carriage. The first thing we noticed and appreciated was how wonderfully warm it was. The lighting, though somewhat dim, was adequate. There were approximately 60 people in the carriage and as far as I could tell, I was the only woman. Each open-ended compartment contained four bunks, two on each side with a window and a small table between. The opposite window had two bunks running parallel to the window.

Of all the contributions the British made to India, the development of the train system was one of the greatest: it changed the life and commercial attitude of its people, forever. In 1853 barely 38 miles of track existed; only 10 years later 5000 miles of steel rolled across the land. It is the second largest railway system in the world under single management; China is the largest. Ten million passengers use the 7000 scheduled services every day and its massive timetables are the most complex on earth. There are 11,160 locomotives, which should be enough to keep any train buff in perpetual heaven. In 1991 there were still 4427 steam trains in service but only about 150 still exist. There are three gauges: broad at 1.67 metres, medium at 1 metre wide and narrow at .0762 metres. The express mail trains travel at an average of 47 kilometres per hour; the passenger trains 27 kilometres per hour. It is always better to try and take an express mail service, unless you like long train rides with numerous stops. The train system employs roughly two million employees, making it the largest boss in the world.

Problems with safety and mismanagement mean some 300 rail accidents in India per year. During the last few years there have been incidents of trains travelling at full speed without a driver: they had apparently either jumped out when the going got rough or fallen out. The worst train accidents in the world have occurred in India. In August 1999, 300 people died when two passengers trains collided head-on.

Although the establishment of the railroad caused dramatic economic changes that would in later years benefit everyone, initially, it caused undreamed of tragedy. For the first time in its history, the rural population, 74 per cent of the India's people, became linked to the port cities of Bombay, Madras and Calcutta. Huge and accelerating demands for raw materials by Britain and other countries meant subsistence farming had to become organised, so commercial agricultural production was introduced. As a first step in this new commercialisation, enormous crops of cotton were grown to supply the Civil War in the United States. The sale of that cotton brought new and undreamed of wealth but when the war ended, Johnny came marching home to plant his own cotton and India was left with a huge surplus. They could not sell the cotton so they had no income, and because they had no income they fell victim to a prolonged and deadly famine that lasted from 1865 until 1900. Tragically compounding the problem, bubonic plague brought into Bombay by infected rats doubled the death rate. From 1895 until 1905 the population went into a decline.

Safely aboard the train, all we wanted was to get some sleep. We pushed our bags under the bottom bunk, Gaston climbed up to the top bed and I arranged my bed as best I could. There was no way I was going to undress with 59 men in the same carriage. I noticed the two men across from us carefully fixing their sheets and getting into their sleeping clothes. The train was comfortable: its wide gauge meant there was very little movement, only a gentle rocking – great for sleeping. There was a toilet at the end of the carriage, it was warm and we were safely on our way at last to Varanasi.

I woke at 7.30 a.m., thankful for several hours of deep sleep. The train had stopped at a village station called Mughalserai. Trying to judge the hours we had been on the train I thought we possibly had an hour or two left before we arrived at Varanasi. Gaston was still asleep. I tentatively asked the man opposite me, now dressed and talking to a friend, if we were anywhere near Varanasi. To my great relief, he spoke English but was uncertain about the distance. I couldn't see

Varanasi

the carriage attendant anywhere. I settled back, combed my hair, tidied up the bedding and relaxed in the early morning sun. A few more men came into our compartment and started talking to the man across from me. I was just thinking how glad I was that Gaston could sleep through it all when one of the men quietly leaned over to me and said, 'Actually, I think this is the stop for Varanasi.' I couldn't even begin to think he might be right. I had no idea how long we had been at the station.

I shook Gaston violently, 'Wake up, wake up. I think we might be at Varanasi!' Rushing into the passageway I tried to find someone who could tell me where we were. Glancing down the platform, all I could see were Japanese tourists. Alarm bells started to ring. There was no way large Japanese groups would be disembarking at some dinky country village. Finally I found a porter who spoke English. 'Yes, this is the stop for Varanasi. The train will be departing in a few minutes.'

'This is it!' I screamed at Gaston. He wasn't even out of his bunk. All I could think of was how we were going to wind up in Bihar, a dangerous place to be at the time. Crazed images flashed through my head of men with long curved moustaches, who carried whips and confiscated passports.

'Are you sure?' Gaston yelled at me. I was tempted to say how could you be sure of anything in India but knew it was too late to reply. I lugged his paintbox out from under the bed and made a wild check for my money belt. I froze. Fingers raced, my heart pounded. During the night it had somehow slipped around my waist and was at my back instead of the front where it should have been. Hoisting my backpack onto my shoulders I shrieked at Gaston, 'Get the black bag and get off the bloody train. We only have seconds left!' Running down the aisle I noticed nearly all the beds were empty. Sandals flapping, I reached the train door. Some kind man helped me down, 'Oh, Madam, better hurry!' It was a 1.5 metre (5 foot) drop to the platform, and difficult with two awkward and heavy pieces of baggage.

I was left standing alone on the platform with half our baggage and no sign of Gaston. It was evident the train was going to go at any second. Should I get back on? How was

I going to get the bags back up the steps? What if the train left while he was still on board? How would we find each other? After what seemed an interminable time but was only seconds, he appeared at the door. As he leapt from the train I could clearly see the angry Flemish swearwords forming on his lips. As his feet hit the pavement, the train left the station. Throwing our arms around each other, we took a deep breath and watched it depart.

Like a lightning bolt, Mr Singh appeared at our side. He had a big, black moustache and a smile that would have cheered up a dog with mange. Mr Singh, taxi driver extraordinaire, informed us he would take us to Varanasi. Within miraculous seconds we had become blood brothers. We hadn't any energy left to withstand him: he had enough for us all. A coolie grabbed our luggage and we were off and running. Swallowed up in a herd of travellers, we were on the move among the hundreds coming in and the hundreds going out. The four of us could have easily passed as a comedy act, a mini band of acrobats and clowns: the two of us, rumpled and pop-eyed, following the gesticulating blue-turbaned Sikh and the porter who laughingly balanced our baggage on his head.

Then, without warning, Mr Singh turned red in the face; his big smile completely drained away. What had happened to our newfound relative? Could he possible be mad at us so soon? Another driver who had spotted us was yelling out that he would take us to Varanasi for 100 rupees less. Fists flew in the air like distress flags on a sinking ship. Mr Singh, shrieking in Hindi, peppered his words with English, the other driver had, 'only' a rickshaw and he had a 'taxi!' Any hope of saving money was squashed by brute, vocal force. Still moving through the throng of people, we were bundled toward an ancient Ambassador car that looked more like a crushed and discarded war tank. The doors were thrown open, and our bodies and baggage flung inside. The coolie's hand floated palm upwards through the open window. The Sikh and the rickshaw driver were still screaming at one another. We sat dazed, frozen into bewilderment. Mr Singh slammed the doors shut, got into the taxi and opened his mouth wide in a toothy grin of triumph and satisfaction. We could never have dreamt that real hysteria was about to begin.

Varanasi

Guru Nanak founded the Sikh religion in 1469 in an attempt to solve the severe problems and conflicts caused by Hinduism and Islam. The idea of a single faceless god, of guru and brotherhood lies at the heart of this religion. "There is no Hindu. There is no Moslem. There is one God, one supreme truth.' The name Sikh comes from the ancient word disciple. There have been ten gurus. The last, Govind Singh, collected all of the former teachings and, adding his own words of love and enlightenment created one book, the *Guru Granth Sahib*, which is an anthology in the form of verses, poems and hymns. The Golden Temple of Amritsar, where the holy book is kept, is the Sikhs' central shrine and their most important place of pilgrimage. Upon entering, each Sikh is given a small portion of holy food that symbolises equality and brotherhood. The Sikh religion was born out of devastating, inhumane treatment of Hindus by the Moslem invaders; the departure from the Hindu religion was a desire to be rid of the caste system and ritualism. By forming a new religion, and taking a stand against both Moslems and Hindus, the Sikhs needed protection for one another, and therefore they became a fighting fraternity. Each devotee was given a new name ending with Singh, meaning lion. (It does not necessarily follow that because a person's last name is Singh he is a Sikh.) Their distinctive appearance was developed as a device for recognising one another and reinforcing their courage to fight for their religion. At puberty, Sikh men begin their lifelong dress code, which is sometimes called the five k's, or kakkars. These are the kirpan, a small sword to defend the defenceless (but now it more likely to be a symbol of a sword); kesh, their hair is left uncut as a symbol of saintliness; kangha, a wooden comb carried in their turban as a sign of cleanliness; kucha, short pants to have the mobility of a warrior; and kara, a steel bangle worn on their right wrist to symbolise determination. When the Mogul Empire collapsed, they seized territory for themselves: their beloved Punjab. They are universally acknowledged not only as skilled drivers and mechanics but some of the world's bravest warriors.

Outside the station in front of the exit gates lay the route to Varanasi, the Grand Trunk Road, which goes from Calcutta via Agra and Mumbai (Bombay). Another road from the north also connects at this junction. Adding bedlam to mayhem was a truck repair area similar to the one just outside Jaipur. Taking the brief slide into hell, we dropped into an abyss of uncontrolled traffic. There was little evidence that, at some time in history, this was a two-lane highway. We were six lanes abreast – four going west and two going east – but it depended entirely upon who had the lead. Mr Singh clearly found the challenge to his taste. His grin got bigger. He rebounded off the seat at every opportunity to overtake another vehicle. His fingers tapped the steering wheel in unbridled impatience if he lost an opportunity to sneak into an inch of space. The engine was flicked on and off as progress dictated. We were rivers of metal, mountains of spilling grain and raw sugar, buildings of buses, all moving together in an extraordinary mass. The air was blue, dense with fumes. The sound of ceaseless horns filled the air like the cacophony of a flock of birds at a watering hole. Mr Singh was now Mr Space Buster. Walls of vehicles encircled us, canyons formed behind us. We were pushed from behind. Car doors made grinding noises against other car doors. Mr Singh, SB was notably extra happy when overtaking looming, leaning Tata trucks or, even better, a bus jammed with helpless passengers. Cramming into the most minuscule of spaces, he would bounce all over the seat and let out a Machiavellian triumphal laugh. After an interminable 40 minutes, and 3 kilometres (1.8 miles), the traffic started to break up. Suddenly we were hurtling through space like a prune pit from a slingshot. By undeniable skill and cunning we careened through herds of buffalo, packs of dogs and frantic bleating goats. The horn of the taxi had beat in a steady coronary distress rhythm from start to finish. Forty-five minutes later we hurtled up a slope to the entrance of the only hotel we knew to ask for, the Hindustani International.

We nearly fell out of the taxi with the sudden loss of momentum and, looking up at the nine-storey, glass-and brass-fronted hotel, we knew we were not going to be able to afford it. Even the cheapest room was just too grand. Gaston was on the verge of enquiring where we might find another place when the clerk asked us that question again. His large brown eyes looked at us patiently and the courteous smile on his face was broken by his words: 'What price would you be being prepared to pay, sir?'

I sat thinking about having to get back into the taxi and possibly another hair-raising ride around town when Gaston suggested 800 rupees. 'Would that be agreeable?'

'I'll ask my manager, sir. We might be able to accept that.' We looked at each other in disbelief and desperate hope. The rooms had air conditioning, a working TV, a good bed and even a bath. It was heaven and there was not a horn in sight. Gaston gave the taxi driver, unforgettable Mr Singh, a tip and thanked him. Under his breath I heard him thank God as well.

Varanasi is the holiest city in India and some say the oldest. The name is derived from the spot where the two rivers, the Varuna and Assi, converge at the Ganges. The Ganges, which flows from south to north, is also known by the old name Kashi, and the more familiar Benaras. Kashi is the permanent home of the god Shiva and it is said that when the world ends Kashi will still survive. It is a city saturated in colour, a mixture of the sacred and the profane, the beautiful and the bizarre. It is the cradle of many religions, originating from a myriad of cultures, and above all it is a city where people come to pray, study, to meditate and die. Seeing the Ganges for the first time makes some sense of the theory that there is no such thing as time: 1000, 2000 years ago, it must have looked nearly the same. As Mecca is to the Moslems, Varanasi is to the Hindu, with the added hope that those who have their ashes thrown in the river here will obtain peace, their cycle of reincarnation will be broken forever and they will have an everlasting death.

By the afternoon we were ready to see the Ganges. Tuk-tuk drivers sat like swarms of mosquitoes at the end of the drive. There are thousands of licensed rickshaw drivers in Varanasi and probably just as many who are not licensed. Not many men own their own vehicles, which makes them vulnerable to exorbitant rental rates from the merchants who control them. We met Parkas, permanently stationed outside the hotel, who became our driver for the rest of our stay. He seemed to understand what we needed. Even if he didn't understand, he would pretend he did, until he did. We wanted to go to the Ganges and see the more than 100 ghats that line the river. Along the road there were as many people walking in the streets as there were on the footpaths. Sacred

A Brush with India

animals impossibly nonchalant, impervious to threats, were not concerned with our needs: we would have to make our way around them. There is a saying about Varanasi that goes, 'The four perils of Kashi are widows, bulls, stairs and holy men. You can only enjoy Kashi if you survive these.'

Puccal Mahal, the ancient home for thousands of people, runs parallel along the high banks of the Ganges and to get to the ghats it is necessary to pass through this area. Our little tuk-tuk managed well but it would not have been possible for a taxi as it was unimaginably congested with narrow tunnel-like streets and an endless labyrinth of passageways. Old buildings three and four storeys high leaned inwards, their overhanging balconies shutting out the sun and the light. Strung from house to house were electricity wires and the remnants of yesterday's festivals. Here, too, animals took refuge: dogs, goats and, of course, mother India its bovine self. Birds' nests crowded into tiny crevices. Replicas of gods and goddesses were painted over every wall. It was impossible to see the river, blocked from view by centuries of successive buildings. An endless sense of movement was created by a moving sea of humanity as people strode with resolute purpose and housewives haggled over prices while merchants tried to beat them down. Hawkers in their hole-in-the-wall shops yelled out, demanding everyone's attention. Carts and vehicles small enough to traverse the tiny lanes somehow hurtled past. The smell of incense, cow dung, warm spicy food and marigold petals permeated the air. Temple worship rang with the noise of drums and bells. Further away we heard the sound of a gong, deep, heavy and resonant. Old men sat on rickety chairs reading newspapers; children stared and gave us slow, shy smiles.

Our first view of the Ganges was too complex to take in. (I have often wondered about tourists who see Europe in 10 days or visit the United States in 12. It must be like being invited to dinner, shown the menu and then have it all whisked away. Only a fleeting glance survives, not a taste or a meaty bite.) In the afternoon light we walked down the steep stairs of a ghat until we reached the water. As far as we could see, in both directions, on cliffs 100 metres above the river, ancient buildings leaned over wide stairs leading down to the Ganges. The skyline was sliced with 5 kilometres (3 miles) of gilded temple pinnacles and oyster-coloured palaces, decrepit, majestic, and impossible to look away from. Posters plastered over white-washed walls advertised messages in the impossible curlicues of Sanskrit. The light was grey and soft, hazy and luminous. We walked along the stairs trying to comprehend it all. Curious tourists, strangers like ourselves, walked tentatively, awkwardly, stopping to look at such an alien landscape. Priests sitting underneath straw umbrellas were dotted here and there like sentinels, their bodies clothed only in thin white dhotis, their foreheads marked with sandalwood paste and vermilion. Sadhus with long grey streaked beards and matted hair sat naked, chanting endless mantras. Pilgrims were filling pots of water to take to their families back home. Even here cows wandered over the white stone, leaving long brown, blurred stains behind them. Hundreds of small boats of all descriptions and sizes were plying up and down the waterfront. We could walk no more than a few yards without the question, 'Boat? Boat? Good price. Sixty rupee?' Pilgrims and tourists piled into fragile floating wooden structures to see the temples from the middle of the Ganges. We had time. We could do it later. We stopped at a tiny café built into a sandstone wall on a terrace so narrow that the legs of our chairs were in a constant peril of falling off the edge. We drank cold Coca-Cola: it was too hot for chai tea. We sat drinking out of the bottle, silent, muted by so many mysterious sights, so many unknowns.

At 6.30 the next morning Parkas met us at the front of the hotel. We were returning to the ghats so Gaston could do a painting in the early morning light. Parkas was a very calm person with enormous, sad brown eyes; he almost never smiled. He showed us a photo of his two children and his beautiful tiny wife. By 7.30 we had driven through the sleeping city and the Pucca Mahal. We walked quickly through the cool streets, down the lane and through the alley to the tops of the ghats. Parkas carried the paintbox down the steep descending steps and he placed it on the ground as gently as if it were a child. The morning sun was already rising. It made a hard, sharp silhouette against the sky and turned everything steely blue. Shadows revealed occasional splashes of red or pink or orange from women's saris. Gaston found the composition he was looking for and set up his easel. Parkas stayed by his side in curiosity as much as anything else, I suspected. I moved further down, but not so far away that I could not see him, and sat on the steps, wishing again that I was invisible so that I would not intrude on or change anything around me. Even more I wished I had an invisible camera.

At the river's edge, men were washing clothes. Their brown, nearly naked bodies worked in shadow against the sun. This was a commercial laundry and huge piles of washing waited for attention. Each piece was picked up, dipped in the river, soaped, rinsed and slapped against large flat rocks, the sound a rhythmic beat in the morning air. When a piece of clothing was finished, it was stretched out to dry on the stairs.

The regular inhabitants strolled up and down: the mustard-robed sadhus, the semi-naked fakirs, the Brahmans, the widows in white. Varanasi has been a refuge for widows for centuries. Here they wait for their death, to be reunited with their husbands. Homes have been set up for their accommodation but provide little else. Endlessly chanting God's name provides a little food from the priests, but usually the women are reduced to begging. Chai wallahs were preparing for people's thirst with the sweet tea that consoles an empty stomach and tricks it into feeling full. Mangy flea-ridden dogs ran around. Boats drifted silently back and forth, their oars dipping up and down, too far away to be heard. Large crowds of worshippers descended the steps, so close I could have reached out and touched them. I, thankfully, did not exist for them; only the Ganges held their attention. 'Har Har Mahadev' – glory to Shiva – and 'Ganga Maiya ki Jai' – glory to Mother Ganga – were repeated over and over as if they were most tender love songs. The sun's rays, a little lower now, were reflected in tight white pools on the water. Swallows were leaving their nests. The worshippers descended toward the water, relatives, friends, and close family. This was a village affair, a family affair, and a time of great celebration. Husbands reached for their wives' hands as they descended together into the river. They removed some of their clothing. The women gracefully twisted and turned in their saris, leaving gossamer lengths of immaculate colour floating on the skin of the Ganges. The water was cold but they did not flinch. Instead, they scooped up the water and trembled with the thrill of it. They smiled and touched it to their foreheads with deep and tender reverence. They were euphoric. As they rose from the Ganges, they laid out their clothing to dry and sat in long lines on the steps. I saw pairs upon pairs of women's diminutive feet, adorned with silver rings on nearly every toe, the privilege of married women. The soft tinkle of bracelets added its song to the more distant sound of conch shells and temple bells. The worshippers moved a few steps higher and were joined by several young priests who began to chant invocations from the Rig-Veda. They paid obeisance to Ganga, the mother, the nourisher and sustainer of all living beings, the river of life.

The atmosphere of devotion, of belief, was unmistakable. Ascetics, to free themselves from worldly sensation and temptation, put into practice tasks of steely concentration. The sight of men lying on beds of nails was commonplace. Another stood for hours with one leg raised and two arms outstretched, like a living coathanger. Not physically agonising but mentally challenging, others sat in trances for hours exploring their mental capacities, searching for answers to the mysteries of man and his place on earth.

Another celebrated religion had its beginning here in Varanasi. As a child growing up in San Francisco, one of my favourite places to play was the Japanese Tea Garden in the Golden Gate Park. I would pack my lunch of sandwiches and a drink of Kool-Aid and sit on top of a high-arched, brown wooden bridge, overlooking the lotus pond. From there I could see the purple irises and water lilies and a little further on an enormous stone statue of a man. I knew the statue was called Buddha and I was sure he was someone very important. I wrongly thought he must be Japanese as he was in my garden. I also thought he must have eaten an awful lot of peanut butter and jelly sandwiches.

So it was a revelation to me that the founder of Buddhism came from northern India. Siddhartha Gautama was born sometime in the sixth century BC, probably 567. He was the son of a lord and rich nobleman from the foothills of the Himalayan mountains. Gautama was an excellent student,

A Brush with India

a great athlete and handsome. He had won the hand of a desired and beautiful princess and very soon they had a son. All his life, owing to the early predictions of an astrologer, Gautama was protected from hardship: even the sight of it was forbidden to his view. Then, one day, he saw four things – the Four Insights, as they are called – that changed him forever: an old man, bent and frail; a man suffering from open sores who trembled and shook with fever; a man who had died; and a beggar whose only possession was his yellow robe and begging bowl but was apparently happy. It was the beginning of the Great Renunciation. Gautama was 29 years old.

A few days later, in the dark of night, enlisting the help of a guard and charioteer, he secretly departed. Fearing he would not have the strength of his beliefs, he dared not looked back. As they came to the cover of the forest, he gave his beautiful silk clothing to his attendant and put on a simple length of cloth. He shaved his hair and sent his locks back to his family so that they might have a last memento of him. His beloved horse was taken back to the palace and, it is said, died from grief a few weeks later. But looking for peace by withdrawing from the world was not as easy as Gautama had imagined. The teachings of other gurus did not leave him peaceful and seeking salvation from a life of austerity left him still unfulfilled. He decided to join five others, like himself, and they retreated to the forest. He imposed ever more difficult regimes on himself, eating only one bean a day. He became so thin he could touch his backbone through his stomach. When he was dangerously emaciated and close to death, a young woman took pity on him and fed him until he recovered. Even this did not lead to enlightenment. His companions, finding him no help for their own enlightenment, wandered away.

He was determined to try again. This time he resigned himself to death if he could not find the knowledge he was looking for. Settling himself down under a fig tree outside the town of Sarnath, he went into a deep trance. At the end of 49 days he opened his eyes and saw the condition of the world with godlike clarity. Finally, after six years, he had received his Great Enlightenment. Thereafter he was called Buddha, the enlightened one.

Buddha's first sermon is one of the most celebrated in

history. It is known as the Four Noble Truths: that all life is suffering, that the cause of suffering is desire, that the end of desire means an end of suffering and that suffering can be stopped by following the Eightfold Path. The path is right views, aspirations, speech, conduct, living, effort, mindfulness and meditation. These views are incorporated in the Middle Way, which avoids both living for pleasure or too much self-denial.

Buddha taught that one is continually reborn into one of six realms of existence. The realm you are born in depends on how well you have behaved in your previous life. This is the meaning of karma. Your next life, for better or for worse, depends entirely on your daily actions in this life. The only way to escape the never-ending cycle of a rebirth is to find the state of happiness, peace and enlightenment known as Nirvana.

Although Buddhism is similar to Hinduism, there are major differences. Buddha refused to engage in abstract speculation about the universe and the result is a religion without a god, without worship, even without a human soul. Hinduism had so many gods they can scarcely be counted. Buddhism believes in rebirth, Hinduism in reincarnation. Buddhism in its original form had no priests. Its teachings were by monks seeking enlightenment through discussion and reasoning. Hinduism had an entire caste of priests and at the time of Buddha taught in arcane Sanskrit, just as the Catholic church used to preach in Latin. Buddhism has, unlike the Hindu, no complex rituals. Nirvana is attainable by everyone, even the Untouchables.

Buddha stayed at Sarnath. His five original followers joined him and to them were added 54 friends. They became the first monks. From there, almost within walking distance of the great ghats of Varanasi, he sent his first monks out into the world to share with others the tenets of his beliefs. Each monsoon season they returned to meditate. Throughout his life he refused to be deified. After his death the sect split into many different branches. Buddhism has spread all over the world but strangely has almost disappeared in India, accounting for less than 1 per cent of the population. Its finest principles were not, however, lost and worked to develop Hinduism into a more tolerant religion.

A Brush with India

It was time for us to go. Gaston had finished the painting, his personal view captured on canvas. We climbed back into the tuk-tuk and returned to the hotel. The painting was placed by the window to dry. 'A View of the Ganges' will always be for me rows of jewelled toes and radiant faces, a sun rising, the washermen of the river.

In the afternoon I went out with Parkas to look for Benaras silk. Caravans on the ancient Silk Road between the East and West spoke of fine material famous for its delicate weave, colour and texture. There were as many merchants as there were pilgrims who made the long journey to Benaras, as it was then called. Silk brocades, silk blends and pure cotton were all just as highly prized hundreds of years ago as they are today, and weavers constantly experimenting with new techniques and motifs have continued to achieve awards. Parkas took me to an establishment that specialised in silk. I suspected it also specialised in fleecing tourists, but I wanted to look anyway. I cannot imagine any cloth more beautiful than the silk I saw. Every diminutive hue was represented in glowing colour. Some shawls were so fine they felt oddly warm to the touch and clung to my fingers like living things. When I asked if it were possible to see the weavers I was shown a well-dressed young man in an immaculate room. He had excellent light and was using an elaborate loom. Jewel-like colours flooded the floor. I knew it wasn't real, just a tourist-mirage. The best weavers in Varanasi are Moslems who start to learn their craft when they are about 11 years old.

The next morning a newspaper was delivered to our room and for the first time since we left home we lay in bed, reading leisurely like most people do on a Sunday. Home seemed so far away. After a light breakfast we went for a walk along the streets outside our hotel. Varanasi is famous for its sweets and we saw them everywhere, being prepared on the sidewalks: hot crisp jelebis that dripped oil and sugar were quickly passed from hand to mouth; chum-chum, ladoos and murraba, the Indian marmalade, formed mountains of potential gratification for the sweet-toothed. We watched the special preparation of paan. After careful consideration a betel nut leaf was selected and laid flat on the table. It was then spread with a mixture of fragrant paste, lime, cardamom, fennel seed and a jelly of rose petals and sugar syrup. The little boat of pleasure was finally topped off with a pinch of tobacco and was ready to be popped into the mouth. I later regretted my reticence and wished I had tried it. At the same spot families went about their business of cutting hair and selling milk in open-fronted shops. Filthy children wearing remnants of clothing played alongside the pigs in the garbage dumped outside the local restaurants. Their mothers had carefully pencilled their eyelids in kohl but little fingers had smudged them making them look as if they had just woken up. I held countless tiny, sticky hands and repeated again and again, 'Hallow, hallow.' Angelic smiles and a sweetness that only children know how to bestow blotted out the dismal truths. They might never be educated or have the right foods they needed for strong growth. They might be dead from disease or amoebic dysentery before they were 10. But right there and at that moment all we saw were children, radiantly beautiful in their simple delight in life.

We returned to our hotel for lunch. We walked over black marble floors, swept and polished, impossibly clean. We sat at a table with a white tablecloth and layers of silverware. Men in white uniforms addressed us as sir or ma'am. I thought of our home where curtains were drawn across its now silent world of carpets and paintings and wardrobes of clothes and a kitchen of copper pans and sets of matching crockery. I thought of shelves of family photos and boxes of Christmas decorations. I sat looking at our lunch of plump chicken with its delicate cashew sauce and stuffed croquette potatoes. Eating such a plate of food seemed humbling; leaving it seemed wasteful.

Today would be Gaston's last painting. When we arrived, we made a turn to the left, opposite our previous journeys to the ghats, and he began the process of setting up his easel, a juggling act perfected over 60 years. Balancing the heavy box against one leg, pulling the three legs out, turning the screws just right, adjusting the height, takes only a few minutes. He screws the canvas into place: sometimes it is snow-white, but usually it is prepared in advance with a pale ochre wash. People began to gather but he goes about his work as if no one is there. Next, he adds additional paint to the full range of colours on his palette and gets out his brushes. He puts on his painting coat and is ready to work. He has already sized up his subject, he knows what he is going to paint: only the final composition is to be decided. He draws the cardboard viewer to his eye, working it forward and back to define and confirm his choice. Waiting a few moments to adjust his eyes, he begins. After six decades of painting, his movements are fluid, his painting statements positive. Indecision over technique has long ceased to be an issue. The mixing of colours is so imprinted in his working habits that he hardly looks at his palette when applying the paint. Ten years ago when he still smoked, his cigar was the only indication of equivocation. The cigar would bob up and down ever so slightly as he had a closer look at his subject. I know the sounds of progress without looking. I can hear a block away the gentle tap of brushes laid down, different from those set aside. The tissue pulled from its box to clean brushes makes a hushing sound, sharp and short. It is the time to talk to him if I want to. But even then, he goes on thinking, creating and unless he looks as if he wants something, it is better to say nothing. Sometimes, I cannot help myself and make it known to others who watch, with some gesture of familiarity, that I belong to him or he belongs to me, whichever way that works. My admiration and love spill over into the egotistical cup of demonstration and possession.

We were standing on top of a large square concrete platform. It had small rails on its outer edge and looked over a drop into the Ganges, 4.5 metres (15 feet) below. The water was brackish, dark and covered in confetti of unknown flotsam. It was late afternoon, and there were only a few people sitting on the steps chatting. Two old men were playing cards. At this end of the ghats it was quieter. The razzmatazz of symbols, the continuous sound of the conch shells and the endless chanting of vedas were heard only as a muffled reminder of other people further up toward the bridge. I waited, as I usually do, to make sure everything was right, that Gaston had decided this was the place where he wanted to stay. In the afternoon light the sky had a faded purple tinge with long ribbons of pink streamers. The buildings silhouetted high against the skyline were a soft turquoise colour. I could see why he had chosen this place.

I had been standing, waiting, looking across the Ganges for some five or ten minutes before I went to look at the fires burning directly on the western side of the concrete platform. At first I did not realise what I was looking at. Then slowly I understood they were burning human bodies. Below the confines of Gaston's painting, out of sight of his viewer, was one of the oldest cremation ghats of the Ganges, the Harishchandra Ghat.

A person who dies at Varanasi and has his ashes thrown in the Ganges is guaranteed to be liberated from the endless cycle of reincarnation. A man's final journey is concluded here. Bamboo stretchers bearing bodies of men wrapped in white shrouds, women in red shrouds and the elderly in gold are a common sight in the narrow alleyways leading down to the river. 'Ram Nam Satya Hai' – the only truth is God's name – rings out like a common greeting. One simply makes way for the dead to pass. For the citizens of Varanasi this is an everyday event, accepted philosophically. This is what their city is about and because death is common, so is rejoicing. The Varanasi residents are extremely proud of their city. They love pleasure and abandonment. To them, everything worth living and dying for is held within its boundaries. Their city not only ensures happiness, but also salvation by release from reincarnation.

There are special places of worship in Varanasi where those who are on the verge of dying can spend their last days. Free board is offered for a limited time but relatives must supply everything else such as medicines and food. Austere but safe, such places provide an atmosphere that invites a peaceful passing. Attendants throughout the day chant the name of God. When a person dies, they are quietly laid out on the floor and sacred tulsi leaves and water from the Ganges are put into their mouth. Here, death is not a cause for grief. The Westerner dies in hope of everlasting life, the Hindu in the hope of death, an end to the endless cycle of reincarnation.

According to the Hindu religion, the goddess Parvati threw herself into the sacrificial fire of her father's house. Her husband Shiva, grief-stricken, carried her charred remains to his home on Mount Kailash. But unknown to Shiva, Parvati's ruby earrings had fallen into the ashes and had been secretly stolen by some Brahmin priests. When Shiva found out, he was so angry he cursed them forever. Their descendants, called doms, manage and control the cremation ghats to this day. They are generally despised as a lowly class and shunned by all.

Fascinated, but unsure whether it was appropriate to watch the funeral pyres, I sat on the stairs at a respectful distance. I didn't know who he was when he first sat beside me. He had oily, slicked back hair, dark skin, yellow eyes and a mouth, that was bloody red from chewing paan. He smelled strongly of garlic.

'It takes three hours for a body to burn,' he said. The dom, the funeral director, was eager to tell me all. His face was as riveting as the fires, just as macabre and just as compelling. Parkas moved toward me and sat next to me. He had the same look that Dinesh used to get when he was not pleased. He whispered to me, 'Not good man.' A dom charges heavy fees for his cremation services and is well known for rummaging through ashes to find jewellery or other precious items. He and his relatives make a handsome living by way of cash, kind and even donation of land in exchange for the price of wood and a funeral on the Ganges. I listened and watched while the children of the dom's family ran in and out among the fires. Dogs rambled by, cows sat near for warmth. The dom knew I was fascinated. He talked slowly, piquing my interest and, as usual, peppering his words with pleas for money 'for the poor'.

He said, 'People who die on other side of the river never attain salvation and reincarnation is in the form of a donkey. Bamboo poles are thrown into the river for pigeons, so they may rest and drink from the river'. The belief is that the bird may be a reincarnated ancestor and the pole will keep it from landing on the other side and reincarnating into something worse than a bird.

Unbelievably, it takes 365 kilos (803 pounds) of wood to completely burn a body. How many kilos of wood are there in a tree? The fires of Varanasi burn day and night, 365 days a year and in several ghats. How many forests does it go through in a week? How long can it continue? Just above the burning fires is a huge diesel fuel crematorium built to save wood and stop further pollution of the Ganges. 'Proper Hindu does not want. Proper Hindu wants cremation with wood lit by sacred fire. How can Ganga, the Purifier become polluted herself?' Well, yes he would put it that way to both intimidate the religious and to make sure he would sell them more wood. So the crematorium remains unused, an ugly duckling that no one wants.

Rotten teeth broken and unattended, swam in red saliva, and a small one-sided smile continually threatened his dark face. Hidden behind his direct, jaundiced gaze was something I could not quite guess. It was more than money, the wish to sell me something. Was it a perverse desire to disgust me by what he said? I never felt repelled. Death is a natural event, as normal as birth. What matters is that it should be peaceful with those you love at your side. I was merely intrigued: was this a better way of doing things?

And so we sat side by side, this dirty, sly, ghoulish man and I. Parkas went back to Gaston. Another stretcher, another body wrapped in gold, was brought down to the burning area. Only men attend a cremation. There was once a good reason for this but it is now outdated since sati is against the law. Years ago there was always the temptation for the selfless widow to jump into the fire and follow her husband to his afterlife, so women were banned from attending. The women also put added stress on everyone because of their emotional reactions. There are five categories of human remains that are not cremated: a person who has died of smallpox, one who had been bitten by a snake, a leper, a saddhu and children aged under 10. These exceptions are weighted with rocks and consigned to the Ganges. Also those who are paupers and cannot afford the wood are sometimes buried in this way. It wasn't long ago that turtles in the river used to nibble at the corpses but they have all been captured.

The solid wood logs for a funeral pyre are laid matchstick fashion, two one way and two the other. The body is placed on top of three layers of wood. The hands and face are uncovered and water from the Ganges is poured over the shoulders and into the mouth. A chosen relative from the family applies ghee, first to the body and then to the surrounding wood to help it burn faster. At the top of the stairs there is a large container about 1.8 metres (6 feet) square where the eternal

A Brush with India

flame is held. Kept alive for hundreds of years, the embers continue to be the sacred source for lighting funeral pyres. A match would be considered profane. After adding another three layers of wood on top of the body, the lonely relative lights the pyre. Just before he cracks the skull to release the soul from human bondage. It is all done quietly, gently and with tenderness.

On the day I was there the male relatives sat mute on the steps, their bodies tight, their large, melancholy eyes looking in only one direction. The fire shot into the air. I tried to imagine what this would be like for me if it were my father, my mother or my husband. It was the most profound of statements on the finality and frailty of life. The fire became an inferno as the top layers of wood yielded their form, their waning life and then disappeared. The body, alight from head to foot, made sizzling noises from the evaporation of blood, mucus and cells. The body exposed, the muscles were relieved of their lifelong written contracts and responded with freedom. The arms lifted straight up and reached out, as if the soul had sighted final death. The eyes were splashes of flames that leaped from the face. These were the only disquieting moments. Noticeably, there was no smell. As the fluids dried, the muscle burned away and only the framework was left. The hipbones and the skull were the last to yield. After three hours the heavy weight of wood and body, reduced to a small bucket of warm ash, would be gathered and given to Mother Ganges, who received it into her flowing veins.

For the next 13 days the relatives would grieve and practise great austerity. The relative who attended to the cremation would be treated as a pariah. All the men would shave their hair. With the help of Brahmin priests they would go through delicate and complicated rituals to ensure the deliverance of the dead man's soul. The women would cut their finger-nails and toe-nails. Special food would be made, particularly rice and black sesame seed balls. If the crows ate them, the freedom of the soul of the departed would be ensured.

The dom took me up the stairs to show me the sacred fire. We walked further into the streets behind the crematorium, streets that looked the same as they must have looked hundreds years ago and longer. The road was unpaved and deeply rutted.

Lining the street were the familiar bamboo litters, with their packages of white, red and gold. When I said I wanted to go back he urged me on to see the silk weavers. I was drifting from diplomatic to curt but, as it turned out, I was glad I went because I found a truth, a truth so much harder to bear than the funeral pyres. It was a truth I had read about but not wanted to believe. I looked through a window in a dark alley and saw a frail boy, about nine years old, sitting and working in a pit. In the gloom one naked bulb over his head gave very poor light. The room was a damp, claustrophobic brick chamber; his clothing was sticking to his arms. He didn't see me. His entire attention was focused on a loom of jewel-coloured silk.

I stepped quickly from the alley and ran straight into Parkas who had come looking for me. He took my hand and we walked quickly back to the ghat. We didn't speak but I knew what he would have said. Gaston was packing up, his work finished. We struggled to move, as if the events of the day weighed us down. We walked further up to another ghat and sat for a few moments on the edge of the river watching young girls make tiny boats of leaves and marigolds, each to be sent out into the river, sailboat wishes to be bought for a few rupees. I took off my sandals and let Mother Ganges caress my toes.

It was time for us to leave. This would be our last train ride in India and the completion of our journey. We boarded this time during daylight for the long overnight trip from Varanasi to New Delhi. Again it was a sleeper car and again I was the only woman. Now that it was time to leave, I was getting used to these sorts of situations. Our compartment window had been struck by something that had caused the glass to haze into thousands of cracks. It was intact but we could not see out. I just couldn't accept that my last look at India would be taken away. When the train was on its way, I walked down to the connection between the two carriages where a young attendant sat perched on top of his bedroll. He didn't speak English but we communicated in the usual simple way of hand signals and smiles. I pointed to the closed railway door and looked out through the small window. The steel plates connecting the wagons moved under my feet like two different earthquakes. Strong acid smells of urine and grinding metal drifted upwards. The attendant smiled again and understood. He opened the doors on both sides and the sudden influx of sunlit air circled around me in a warm embrace. As the doors opened another smell, of earth and fields, of mustard and wild flowers, came rushing forward.

The farmland going north from Varanasi was beautiful at the beginning of March. The tall, slender, golden heads of wheat billowed gently from the momentum of the train. The full puffs of white cotton, with their scrappy brown edges, were beginning to outgrow the fragile frameworks that had sent them high above the ground. Man-made ponds held naked children, swimming and throwing water at each another, as children do everywhere. Their mothers stood nearby in their technicolor dresses, hands folded over swelling stomachs. Herds of buffalo were sitting under trees, endlessly chewing their ochre-coloured chaff. Big, pink tongues, warm and wet, seemed to consider each blade as if looking for some new taste. Farmers returning home smiled and waved to this stranger on the train. It all seemed so serene, so normal. How could I have ever sensed the secret anguish?

This is how the world is, now that so many of us have the freedom, the money and the ability to peek into its every corner. It makes us feel good to see 'the culture' to feel we might have learnt something. But it is an illusion – at best a sepia wash, a loose sketch.

Three months later I would read about fields just like these, their blossoming promise turned to disaster. El Niño doesn't give a fig about boundaries. Rain when there should not have been rain and none when there should have been had turned those farms into dust bowls filled with plagues of insects. Even as our train hurtled toward New Delhi it was too late for some. Indian farmers were already swallowing poisons that were too feeble to protect their crops, but strong enough to kill a man. The numbers of deaths would be unprecedented. Normally a respite of a year or two lets the farmers recover but several years of catastrophes in the farmlands have given no relief. Land is so precious in India. The preservation of a man's land for his family and his dignity are paramount. Everything is sacrificed to keep it: a woman's dowry, her only earrings, the last cow, the food reserved for the winter and finally even the door of the house. When, at last, the farmer has no more, he resorts to the moneylenders. Too late for normal resources, when banks will no longer lend, the unscrupulous crooks, the 'cheaters', move in for the bones. They charge up to 98 per cent interest on loans and in the end the farmer feels he has only one choice: suicide. At least by giving up his life he might be able to save the land and his family. The government has tried to help by giving widows enough money to discharge their debts and send their children to school, free of charge, but clearing loans is only for those who have gone through normal sources such as banks and whose dead family member belonged to the present political party. Small landowners usually cannot get loans and are at the mercy of every moneylender and crook who sells them watered-down pesticides and bad seeds.

The train continued mile after mile through evening light streaked with deep triangles of sunlight – blood-red, orange and purple. As we arrived at a station and came to a slow stop I leaned out of the carriage door. Scattered everywhere along the tracks were little clay cups, broken, discarded. I had never noticed them before and wondered what they were doing there. I moved to the other side, open along the quay. There was no one around. A chai wallah with all his paraphernalia approached. He nodded and raised his hand and eyebrows in expectation of a sale. I smiled back and nodded a no. I would have liked a drink but was unsure of how much it was or if he spoke English. Would we have time to drink it? Would it come in one of those filthy glasses as it does in South America? It seemed all too complicated. He continued along the quay.

The attendant and I rested a little from the noise and endless clatter as the train remained in the station. Before long, the chai wallah was on his way back and coming toward us. His smile was as warming as the afternoon sun. In one hand was a steaming aluminium kettle, in the other a little clay cup. He poured the milky liquid into it and passed it up to me, then another for the attendant. It was his gift to us, kindly offered with no thought of reward. He could not have known that I saw it as a farewell gift or why it brought tears to my eyes. I had been humbled once again by the simple kindness of the people of India.

India is so large and so diverse that one could only ever have a small taste of its culture and its land. Whether you love it or hate it, the memory of its people and the paradox of their poverty and generosity will remain with you forever. Black or white, true or false – these are Western inventions. India is every shade of grey that ever existed. The only absolute truth is that there is no such thing.

Epilogue

IN THE MONTHS THAT followed our return home I started to read book after book about India. I read them with intensity. In all our travels I had never experienced such a drive to know more. To this day I feel the same, a book, a film and television program about India draws me irresistibly to the same subject.

India has changed the way I think about life. It is not that I have converted to a new religion like Hindu or Moslem, or even that I am counting the days until we return. It is more the way India opened my eyes to comparisons and new ideas. Every day I have so much to be thankful about, our children, our loved ones, our house, our work, our rewards and that we have one another. I knew all those things before, but after seeing India I was overwhelmed by our chance in life. I look at my grandchildren and I know they will never suffer from a lack of education or near starvation. In the food that we eat I am aware of its variety and abundance. In my home I see the luxury that so many cannot dream of. I now accept these things with a grateful heart and with a bowed head.

And what of things like religion and politics? The pleasure to read about the doctrines of the Hindu, the Moslem, the Buddhist, and Christians by contrast was to come to the realisation that they are all remarkably similar. It gives me a sense of peace and a place to start. Politics are generally a subject far from my inquisitions but even in this, India educated me and led me from question to question. I now understand the enormous difference and distrust between Hindus and the Moslems, therefore I understand Kashmir. I now understand Pakistan and their conflict between politics and religion and their dilemma. So it is an easy stepping-stone to Afghanistan.

India has given me a deeper understanding of life by the simple merits of comparison and a common language. I hope this book will serve not only as a profound thank you to the people of India but also as an enticement for those who read it to experience India for themselves.

Linda-Marie De Vel,
Orewa, NZ